Turabian: The Easy Way!

Peggy M. Houghton, Ph.D.
Timothy J. Houghton, Ph.D.

Editor: Michele M. Pratt

Education is one of the best investments you will ever make…and our books maximize that investment!
Houghton & Houghton

Baker College
Flint, MI

ISBN: 978-0-923568-91-7

For more information, contact:

Baker College Bookstore
bookstore@baker.edu
800-339-9879

LIBRARY OF CONGRESS CATALOGING-IN-PUBLICATION DATA

Houghton, Peggy M.
  Turabian : the easy way! / Peggy M. Houghton, Timothy J. Houghton ; editor, Michele M. Pratt.
    p. cm.
  "The intent of this handbook is simply to supplement the official A Manual for Writers of Research Papers, Theses, and Dissertations (7th edition)"--Pref.
  Includes bibliographical references and index.
  ISBN 978-0-923568-91-7
  1. Dissertations, Academic--Handbooks, manuals, etc. 2. Academic writing--Handbooks, manuals, etc. I. Houghton, Timothy J., 1961- II. Pratt, Michele M. III. Turabian, Kate L. Manual for writers of research papers, theses, and dissertations. IV. Title.

  LB2369.H69 2008
  808'.02--dc22
                                      2008048820

Manufactured in the United States of America

Table of Contents

Preface   iv

Part One: Mechanics of Turabian   1

**Part Two: Planning, Drafting, & Revising the Research
       Document**   7
   Finding Appropriate Sources   7
   The First Draft   8
   Avoiding Plagiarism   9

Part Three: Punctuation and Style   13
   Spelling and Punctuation   13
   Names and Terms   19
   Numbers   24
   Abbreviations   27
   Quotations   30
   Illustrations   34

Part Four: Source Citation   41
   Citation Styles   41
   Notes and Bibliography System   44
   Author-Date System   57
   Coding System   61
   Books   61
   Periodicals   71
   Reviews   79
   Interviews   80
   Unpublished Works   82
   Special References   85
   Audiovisual Materials   88
   Legal Citations   90
   Public Documents   93

Part Four: Sample Paper   97

Index   107

Preface

With more than 35 years of teaching experience, the authors of this handbook have learned that there has been considerable confusion with writing according to Turabian guidelines. Those who are familiar with Turabian format realize that many students and writers are apprehensive and rather perplexed with this particular writing style.

Turabian writing style is designed for colleges, universities, and those who intend to publish. Many adhere to these stringent guidelines. Years of experience have proven that there are consistent questions and misunderstandings regarding the style. Consequently, this document has been developed to simplify the Turabian writing experience. There are some Turabian points that are optional; therefore, the instructor or journal editor should be consulted for final authority with regard to all writing assignments.

The intent of this handbook is simply to supplement the official *A Manual for Writers of Research Papers, Theses, and Dissertations* (7th edition). It is provided as a condensed version of the actual manual. It is not intended to supersede the manual, rather reduce its complexity. This explains the title: *Turabian: The Easy Way!*

The handbook is divided into five parts. Part one focuses on the mechanics of Turabian style writing; part two emphasizes planning, drafting, and revising a research document; part three describes punctuation and writing style; part four explains source citations; and part five provides a sample paper.

Note: Throughout this document, single-spacing has been utilized. Although this is not in accordance with Turabian writing style, it has been used to simply save space. In addition, some names given throughout are fictitious.

Part One
Mechanics of Turabian

Utilizing Microsoft Word (for applications prior to Microsoft Word 2007)

The following are specific instructions on how to set up a Turabian document using Microsoft Word.

Margins

All margins (top, bottom, and sides) should be set at least one inch. Microsoft Word allows the user to set the margin at a default of one inch. To do so, follow the guidelines below:

1. Under FILE, select PAGE SETUP.

2. Select MARGINS tab and type 1" at TOP, BOTTOM, LEFT, and RIGHT boxes. Click OK.

Alignment/Line Spacing

All documents following Turabian guidelines are required to be left aligned and generally double-spaced throughout the entire document (see below for exceptions). Be sure not to include additional spacing between paragraphs, headings, etc. To set the default, follow these guidelines:

1. Place the cursor at the start of the document; select FORMAT.

2. Under FORMAT, select PARAGRAPH.

3. Under PARAGRAPH, set ALIGNMENT to LEFT.

4. Under PARAGRAPH, set LINE SPACING to DOUBLE. Click OK.

The following items should be single-spaced:

1. Block quotations

2. Table titles and figure captions

The following should be internally typed single-spaced but with a blank line between items:

1. Specific elements in the front matter, such as the table of contents and lists of figures, tables, and abbreviations

2. Footnotes or endnotes

3. Bibliographies or reference lists

Font Type and Size

The entire document should be developed using the same font type and size. The actual font type and font size in Turabian should be an easy-to-read font such as 10 or 12-point Times New Roman or Palatino and should be used throughout the entire document. To set both the font size and style using Word, do the following:

1. Under FORMAT, select FONT.

2. Under FONT, select Times New Roman or Palatino.

3. Under SIZE, select 10 or 12. Click OK.

This is an example of 12-point Times New Roman.

This is an example of 12-point Palatino.

Spacing and Paragraph Indentation

Insert only one space (not two) following all terminal punctuation of a sentence using Turabian format style. All papers typed in this format should use the tab key for indentation. Be sure to indent all paragraphs consistently. This can be accomplished by simply striking TAB on the keyboard.

To set tab to the one-half inch default, do the following:

1. Under FORMAT, select PARAGRAPH.

2. Under PARAGRAPH, select TABS.

3. Under TABS, set DEFAULT TAB STOPS at .5". Click OK.

Hanging Indents

To set the hanging indent feature, do the following:

1. Under FORMAT, select PARAGRAPH.

2. Under SPECIAL, choose HANGING. Click OK.

Page Numbering

Page numbering should begin with page two (2) on the first page *after* the title page. The title page does not contain a page number. Page numbering should appear one-half inch down from the top margin. The actual location of the page numbers can be located in one of three places: centered in the footer (at the bottom of the page), centered in the header (at the top of the page), or flush right in the header. This can be accomplished using the HEADER AND FOOTER function. To place the page numbering in the upper right-hand corner, follow these instructions:

1. Under VIEW, select HEADER AND FOOTER.

2. Select the page number icon (the first icon on the left with the # symbol); the number will appear on the left side. The cursor will appear to the right of the number. Move the cursor, using the left arrow key, to the left of the number.

3. Highlight the number.

4. Click the align right key located in the toolbar.

5. Click CLOSE.

6. Under INSERT, select PAGE NUMBERS. Uncheck SHOW PAGE NUMBER ON FIRST PAGE. Click CLOSE.

Whatever location is selected, it should be followed consistently throughout the document for use with classroom papers.

Utilizing Microsoft Word 2007

The following are specific instructions on how to set up a Turabian document using Microsoft Word 2007.

Margins

Margins

1. Select PAGE LAYOUT from the ribbon tabs.

2. Select the MARGINS icon from the PAGE SETUP drop-down menu.

3. Select CUSTOM MARGINS. Type 1" for the TOP, RIGHT, LEFT, and BOTTOM margins. Before leaving this setup, select APPLY TO: Whole Document, then click OK.

Alignment/Line Spacing

Alignment/ Line Spacing

1. Select HOME from the ribbon tabs.

2. Select the PARAGRAPH tab window, and choose LINE SPACING by selecting the LINE SPACING drop-down arrow.

3. Select LINE SPACING OPTIONS, and select ALIGNMENT LEFT.

4. Select LINE SPACING to DOUBLE, and click OK.

Font Type and Size

Font Type and Size

1. Select HOME from the ribbon tabs.

2. Select the FONT window.

3. Under FONT, select Times New Roman or Palatino.

4. Under SIZE, select 10 or 12. Click OK.

> This is an example of 12-point Times New Roman.
>
> This is an example of 12-point Palatino.

Paragraph Indentation

1. Select HOME from the ribbon tabs.

2. In the PARAGRAPH window, select LINE SPACING and LINE SPACING OPTIONS.

3. At the bottom of the pop-up window, select TABS. Set default TAB STOPS at .5", and click OK.

Paragraph Indentation

Hanging Indents

1. Select HOME from the ribbon tabs.

2. In the PARAGRAPH window, select LINE SPACING and LINE SPACING OPTIONS.

3. Select SPECIAL and choose HANGING; click OK.

Hanging Indents

Page Numbering

Page numbering should begin with page two (2) on the first page *after* the title page. The title page does not contain a page number. Page numbering should appear one-half inch down from the top margin. The actual location of the page numbers can be located in one of three places: centered in the footer (at the bottom of the page), centered in the header (at the top of the page), or flush right in the header. This can be accomplished using the HEADER AND FOOTER function. To place the page numbering in the upper right-hand corner, follow these instructions:

Page Numbering

1. Select INSERT from the ribbon tabs.

2. Select PAGE NUMBERS in the HEADER/FOOTER box.

3. Select TOP OF PAGE and PLAIN NUMBER 3 example.

4. Select the PAGE LAYOUT ribbon tab.

5. Click PAGE SETUP; click LAYOUT tab.

6. Under HEADER/FOOTER, check the box next to DIFFERENT FIRST PAGE. Click OK.

Whatever location is selected, it should be followed consistently throughout the document for use with classroom papers.

Part Two:
Planning, Drafting, and Revising the Research Document

The Beginning

Research typically begins with a question that either the writer or outside readers want answered. Regardless of the research length (i.e. research paper, master's thesis, dissertation, etc.), the process should be well thought out. The writer should not delve into the writing without proper preparation. He or she should begin the research preparation by looking at the "large picture." Authors should brainstorm alone or with others and jot down all ideas that come to mind. Remember, brainstorming is meant to bring out creativity and innovation. Research topics should be documented but should *not* be evaluated until all ideas are listed.

Once the topic or question of the research is developed, then the writing should be broken down into small segments. Each segment can be considered a goal, and each goal should have a plan.

In order to accomplish the individual goals, the researcher should plan to write daily. While much of this writing may not be used in the final draft, the process itself is a good disciplinary action. As with everything, "The more you do it, the better you get!" In the end, research will be evaluated on how well it was developed, reported, and substantiated.

Finding Appropriate Sources

Three types of research exist: *primary, secondary*, and *tertiary*. Basically *primary* is firsthand, *secondary* is secondhand, and *tertiary* is thirdhand data.

Primary research is data collected specifically by the individual conducting the research. It can be used to answer a question, support a claim, substantiate a thought, etc. This type of research can also include other original works such as diaries, letters, manuscripts, or films. It is collected and analyzed for a given study.

Secondary research is data that already exists and has been collected by another source. This type of research is not original, in that the researcher is using another person's work. When using secondary research, appropriate credit must be given to the originating author.

Tertiary, or thirdhand, research is typically based on secondary sources and provides a general overview. Encyclopedias, dictionaries, newspapers, and magazines can be tertiary research sources, provided they have been edited and are considered a legitimate source. As with secondary research, all tertiary research must be properly cited.

Regardless of the research type, both secondary and tertiary resources should be credible. Sources should be evaluated for both relevance and reliability. Relevance simply means that the resource pertains to the topic in which the researcher is studying. Perusing the table of contents, the first chapter, and the index will assist in determining if the resource relates to the writer's study. Reliability, on the other hand, refers to confidence in the resource. Is the author a known scholar? Does the author possess the necessary credentials? Is the article current? Resources that are both relevant and reliable are a critical ingredient of any successful research.

The First Draft

All writers have their own unique writing style. Some people prefer to begin their first draft with an outline. Others may review a list of key words they have developed throughout the planning phase of the research project, and still others may want to use the "brainstorm" approach where they write down any idea that comes to mind so that the writing flow is fluid and continuous. Writing style is a personal preference. The approach that is most comfortable for the writer should be the approach that is utilized.

As noted earlier, there are different types of literature that assist the researcher: primary, secondary, and tertiary. Writers must integrate outside resources with their own original thoughts so that the document is balanced. Fresh thoughts along with paraphrasing and the use of direct quotations produce a solid research document.

The First Draft

Paraphrasing (rewording) is using another's thoughts. The writer may wish to paraphrase when he or she can express the thought more clearly or concisely or when the exact quotation is not necessary to convey the thought as intended in the research. When paraphrasing work from another author, it is imperative that the writer provide credit to the person who developed the original work. This simply acknowledges the fact that the paraphrased material was the work of another individual. It is not primary data (original); rather it is secondary data (information already in existence).

Using direct quotes simply means citing an outside resource exactly as it appears in the original source. Authors may wish to use direct quotes to substantiate their claim, to quote an authority figure, or to convey precise and compelling thoughts. Just as with paraphrasing, when citing a direct quote, appropriate credit must be provided. Again, this signifies that the quote is provided by another individual. When citing verbatim (using another person's exact wording), the borrowed material must be properly cited.

Avoiding Plagiarism

Avoiding Plagiarism

Plagiarism is a growing problem both domestically and internationally. The word *plagiarize* is defined in *Merriam Webster's Collegiate Dictionary* (10th edition) as "to steal and pass off (the ideas or words of another) as one's own" (888).

Plagiarism can take one of two forms: intentional or unintentional. When a writer knowingly uses other authors' works without providing appropriate reference citations, he or she is intentionally plagiarizing. If, on the other hand, a writer uses others' thoughts or ideas and does not realize that credit must be provided, he or she is guilty of unintentional plagiarism. Unfortunately, both types of mistakes can result in serious consequences.

It is incumbent on the writer to be forthright and honest with regard to using original and/or existing writing. Plagiarism can be easily avoided if the writer simply provides appropriate credit when borrowing ideas or citing directly from another individual's work.

Presentation of Tables and Figures

When only a few numbers are included, quantitative data should be presented verbally (written in sentence format). However, if most of the data is quantitative or if there are large sets of data, the data should be conveyed graphically.

Various types of graphics are available to present data. The following are a few examples of graphic possibilities:

Table: Typically used to highlight particular values or units

Bar Chart: Typically used to highlight comparisons

Line Graph: Typically used to highlight trends

The design of tables and figures should be concise and accurate. Computer programs now allow researchers to present graphics in very tech savvy ways. However, sometimes the creativity from these programs results in confusion. It is in the writer's best interest to present data in a clear and meaningful manner.

Revising the Draft

After completing the first draft, it is time to go back and thoroughly edit the document. Some writers feel more comfortable revising a draft document with a hard copy of the paper. They prefer to be able to view the entire document at once as opposed to a page by page process on a computer screen. Others prefer to make their changes by typing directly on the keyboard. They are able to mentally prepare their revisions and physically type their thoughts on the keyboard. There is no right or wrong; it is simply a matter of preference.

To begin the process, consider the body of the paper, or big picture. Evaluate the overall organization of the document. Is the body of the report coherent? Is there a common theme throughout the writing? Continue with reviewing the various paragraphs, sentences, individual wording, spelling, punctuation, and grammar. Move words or paragraphs to revise the writing and make the sentences and paragraphs flow smoothly.

There is much debate regarding the use of first and second-person pronouns in research writing. Many authors vehemently believe that first-person should never be used; others feel there are certain times when first-person is appropriate. The authors of this handbook believe first-person generally should not be used in academic or journal writing. However, be sure to consult with the faculty member or journal editor for final clarification.

Once the body has been revised and finalized, the introduction and conclusion need to be addressed. The introduction is a critical component of any writing. This portion is the reader's first exposure to the document. It should provide a general overview of the research, and it should entice the reader to continue reading. Similarly, the conclusion is also extremely important in the completion of the paper. The conclusion of the document should provide closure to the paper and reinforce the significance of the study.

Part Three:
Punctuation and Style

Spelling

All spelling should be based on American usage. If there are any questions, the writer should consult a dictionary. Two good dictionary sources are the *Webster's Third New International Dictionary* or *Merriam-Webster's Collegiate Dictionary* (11th edition).

Spelling

The computer spellcheck option is a feature that will assist the author. However, the writer must be cognizant of the fact that some errors will not be detected with spellcheck. For example, *there* and *their* are both spelled properly. But the accurate spelling of the word is based on the context, or meaning, of the sentence. As such, the document must be thoroughly reviewed for all possible spelling errors.

Punctuation

Period

A period (.) should be used in the following instances:

Periods

- at the end of a statement or command

- at the end of a polite request or command

- at the end of an indirect question

- with decimals

Comma

A comma (,) should be used in the following instances:

- to set off nonessential expressions: those words not **Commas** necessary to convey the meaning of the sentence

- to set off words, phrases, or clauses when they interrupt the flow of a sentence

- to set off words, phrases, or clauses that dangle at the end of a sentence
- to set off transitional expressions
- to set off descriptive expressions that follow the word(s) they refer to and provide nonessential information
- to separate words, phrases, or clauses within a sentence
- to separate two independent clauses that are connected by a conjunction

Commas

- to separate a dependent clause that precedes an independent clause
- if the dependent clause is nonessential and either follows the main clause or is placed within the main clause
- if words and phrases at the beginning, within, or end of the sentence are nonessential
- with residence and business connections
- in dates
- with Jr., Sr., etc.
- in geographic references and addresses
- in a series

Semicolon

A semicolon (;) should be used in the following instances:

Semi-colons

- between two independent clauses when no conjunction is utilized
- with transitional expressions
- in a series of items which already contain a comma(s)

Colon

A colon (:) should be used in the following instances:

Colons

- between independent clauses when the second clause clarifies the first clause and no conjunction or transitional expression is utilized to link the clauses

- before lists and enumerations
- in expressions of time and proportions
- in business documents
- in reference to books or publications

Question Mark

A question mark (?) should be used in the following instances:

- to indicate direct questions
- to indicate questions within sentences
- to express doubt

Exclamation Point

A exclamation point (!) should be used in the following instance:

- to express strong feeling

Dash

A dash (-) *can* be used in the following instances:

- in place of a comma to show strong emphasis on nonessential elements of the sentence
- in place of a semicolon to show a stronger break between clauses
- in place of a colon to introduce words, phrases, or clauses
- in place of parentheses to give nonessential elements strong emphasis

A dash (-) *should* be used in the following instances:

- to indicate an abrupt break or an afterthought
- to indicate hesitation
- to emphasize a specific word(s)
- with repetitions, restatements, and summarizing words

Notes regarding dashes:

Never use a comma, semicolon, or colon before an opening dash. Additionally, do not use a period before an opening dash unless the period follows an abbreviation.

Unless a period follows an abbreviation, do not use a period before the closing dash when writing a statement or a command that is set off by dashes within a sentence.

Use a question mark or exclamation point before the closing dash when a question or an exclamation is set off by dashes within a sentence.

Dashes

Retain the closing dash and omit the comma when a closing dash occurs at a point where the sentence requires a comma.

Drop the closing dash and use the appropriate sentence punctuation if a closing dash occurs at a point where the sentence requires a semicolon, colon, or closing parenthesis.

Use an *em dash* (a dash as wide as a capital *M*) when typing dashes. The *em dash* is typically included in most software packages. However, if it is not, a dash is constructed by striking the hyphen key **twice** with no spaces between the hyphens. Never use a single hyphen as a dash.

A *two-em dash* indicates that letters are missing from a word; if an *em-dash* is unavailable, use four consecutive hyphens (with no spacing between hyphens). A *three-em* dash indicates that a complete word has been left out or needs to be provided; if an *em-dash* is unavailable, use six consecutive hyphens (with no spacing between hyphens).

Parentheses

Parentheses ( ) should be used in the following instances:

Parentheses

- with explanatory material
- with reference information and directions
- with dates
- with enumerated items

Notes regarding parentheses:

Punctuation that follows a parenthesis (i.e. comma, semicolon, etc.) should be placed *outside* the closing parenthesis.

Unless using an abbreviation, do not use a period before the closing parenthesis.

Only use a question mark or exclamation point before the closing parenthesis if the mark applies specifically to the word(s) enclosed in parentheses *and* the sentence ends with a different mark of punctuation. Otherwise, the punctuation mark should be placed after the closing parenthesis.

If the words in parentheses are to be treated as a *separate sentence*, the preceding sentence should close with the appropriate punctuation mark. The words in parentheses should begin with a capital letter. Punctuation for the sentence enclosed within parentheses should be placed before the closing parenthesis, and no additional punctuation should follow the closing parenthesis.

Quotation Marks

Quotation marks (" ") should be used in the following instances:

- to enclose a direct quotation; direct quotation means exact words of another individual

- with titles of literary and artistic works

Notes regarding quotation marks:

Periods and commas are always placed inside the quotation marks.

Slang expressions and the use of deliberate improper grammar and spelling are enclosed in quotation marks so that the reader understands the writer intentionally made the error(s).

Quotation marks are placed around the titles that represent only *part* of a complete published work (such as article or chapter titles). Titles of *complete published* works (such as books or journals) are italicized. However, quotation marks are placed around the titles of *complete but unpublished* works.

Use quotation marks around the titles of songs and short musical compositions. Additionally, use quotation marks around the titles of individual segments or programs that are part of a TV or radio series.

A quotation within a quotation is enclosed in a pair of single quotation marks.

Semicolons and colons are always placed outside the closing quotation mark.

At the end of a sentence, a question mark or exclamation point is placed *inside* the closing quotation mark when it applies only to the quoted material; at the end of a sentence, a question mark or exclamation point is placed *outside* the closing quotation mark if it applies to the entire sentence.

Quotation Marks

When a quoted sentence is independent (stands alone), the appropriate punctuation is placed *inside* the closing quotation mark.

Omit the period before the closing quotation mark and use a comma instead if the quoted statement occurs at the beginning of a sentence. A comma generally precedes the opening quotation mark when a quoted statement, question, or exclamation is located at the end of a sentence and introduced by an expression such as *he said*.

Commas are not required to set off a quotation that occurs within a sentence if the quotation is an essential expression. However, if the quotation is *not* essential to the meaning of the sentence, then it should be set off with commas.

The preferred way to handle a long quotation (five lines or longer) is to indent the quote a half inch from each side margin. The actual quotation should be single-spaced. A blank line should be left above and below the quotation.

Use ellipses marks (. . .) if one or more words are omitted within a quotation. An ellipsis is typed as three periods with one space before and after each period.

Order of Punctuation Marks

Adjacent marks of punctuation typically involve terminal punctuation marks with quotation marks, parentheses, or brackets.

A final comma or period generally precedes a closing quotation mark, regardless of whether or not it is part of the quotation. Question marks and exclamation points precede a closing quotation mark if they are part of the quoted material. However, they are placed after the quotation mark if they apply to the entire sentence in which the quotation appears. Semicolons and colons are always placed after the quotation marks.

If a complete sentence is enclosed within parentheses, place the terminal punctuation (i.e. period, exclamation point, etc.) for that sentence prior to the last parenthesis. However, the terminal punctuation should be placed outside when the material in parentheses is included within another sentence. These guidelines also apply to material placed in brackets.

Personal Names

Capitalization. Both real and fictitious names of individuals are capitalized. Except when initials are used alone, the space between the initials should be the same as the space between the last initial and the name.

Janice Moran	P. K. Roddy	MLK

Hyphenated and extended names. Hyphenated last names or names that consist of two or more elements should include the name(s) in its entirety.

Robert James Worthington	Lynne Morgan-Bernard

Titles and Offices

Capitalization. In general, when civil, military, religious, and professional titles precede a personal name, they are capitalized. However, when these titles follow a name or are used in place of a name, they are lowercased.

President Clinton; the president
James A. Stahley; the dean
Reverend James V. Rubert; the pastor
Pope Benedict XVI; the pope

Academic Designations. Student status and names of degrees are lowercased.

junior	master's degree	doctorate degree

Terms of Respect. The title itself is capitalized. Articles such as *the* that precede the formal name are lowercased.

the Queen Mother	Mr. President

Ethnic, Socioeconomic, and Other Groups

Capitalization. Capitalize the names of national and ethnic groups.

African Americans; African American culture
Caucasians; Caucasian culture

Class. Lowercase lettering is used when denoting socioeconomic classes.

the middle class; middle class classification
the elite; elite classification

Names of Organizations

Capitalization. Full names of legislative, administrative, and judicial bodies are capitalized. Articles such as *the* that precede the formal name are lowercased.

> the House of Representatives; the lower house of Congress
>
> the United States Postal Service; the post office
>
> the United States Supreme Court; the Supreme Court

Institutions and Companies. The full names of institutions and companies (and their respective departments) are capitalized. Articles such as *the* that precede the formal name are lowercased.

> the Library of Congress; the library
>
> the Kroger Corporation; the corporation

Associations and Conferences. The full names of associations and conferences are capitalized. Articles such as *the* that precede the formal name are lowercased.

> the League of Catholic Voters; the league
>
> Global Leadership: Portraits of the Past, Visions for the Future 2009; the conference

Historical and Cultural Terms

Historical Events. Major historical events are capitalized. However, historical events known by their generic descriptions are lowercased. Articles such as *the* that precede the formal name are lowercased.

> the Great Depression   the depression

Sporting Events. Full names of major sporting events should be capitalized. Articles such as *the* that precede the formal name are lowercased.

> the MBA World Championship Series
>
> the championship series

Academic Subjects, Course of Study, and Lecture Series. Unless part of an official course name, academic disciplines are not capitalized. Official course names are capitalized. Names of lecture series are capitalized. Likewise, individual lectures are capitalized and generally enclosed in quotation marks.

Professional development courses are currently being offered at most universities.

Enrollment ends March 17 for Knowledge Management.

The lecture, "How to Make Money in an Economic Downturn," was very well received.

Military Terms

Wars and Revolutions. Major wars and revolutions are capitalized. When using generic terms, lowercased lettering is used.

Iraq War	Vietnam War; the war

Books and Periodicals

"The" in Periodical Titles. When *the* precedes newspaper and periodical titles in text, even if *the* is part of the official title, it is lowercased.

Michigan citizens regularly read the *Detroit News*.

Words to Italicize. Official names of periodicals should be italicized.

Many young people read *People* magazine.

Poems and Plays

Titles of Poems. Quoted titles of poems are usually set in roman type and placed in quotation marks. Poetic work that is exceptionally long, however, is italicized and not placed in quotation marks.

Chaucer's *Canterbury Tales*

First Lines. Poems that are referred to by a first line, as opposed to title, are capitalized in sentence format (according to the capitalization used in the actual poem).

"To Mr. Paul Gaimard"

Titles of Plays. Quoted titles of plays are italicized.

Wilde's *The Importance of Being Earnest*

Unpublished Works

Written Works. Unpublished works such as theses, dissertations, copies of speeches, etc., are placed in roman type, capitalized as titles, and placed in quotation marks. No quotation marks are used with the names of manuscript collections. Titles of soon-to-be published books that are under contract may be italicized, but state *forthcoming* or *in press* in parentheses following the title.

> Correspondence and other material can be found in the Ronald Reagan Collection at the library at the University of Texas.
>
> Houghton & Houghton's *Writing at the College Level* (forthcoming) is due out in September.

Movies, Television, and Radio

What to Italicize. Movie titles, television programs, and radio programs are italicized. A television series' single episode is set in roman and placed in quotation marks.

> *Seinfield* is even more popular in rerun episodes.

Electronic Sources

Analogy to Print. Titles of periodicals or complete works are italicized if information is available on the Internet or in CD-ROM format (even if the information exists in print format). Additionally, articles or sections of works are placed in roman and, when required, placed in quotation marks (even if the information exists in print format).

> *Fortune* is the most popular title.

Online Sources. Book titles are italicized. Titles of articles, poems, short stories, etc., are set in roman and enclosed in quotation marks.

> *Leadership Lessons* was an integral part of my research
>
> "Business Etiquette" is the most read article in the journal.

Musical Works

Musical Works

Long Musical Compositions and Songs. Titles of long musical compositions are italicized. Titles of songs are set in roman, capitalized exactly like poems, and placed in quotation marks.

> *The Indian Queen* is one of the best operas I have ever seen.

Paintings, Graphic Art, and Sculpture

Painting, Graphic Art, and Sculpture

Paintings and Statues. Titles of paintings, statues, and other works of art are italicized. The names of works whose creators are generally unknown are set in roman. Photograph titles are set in roman and placed in quotation marks.

> The *Mona Lisa* is well known.

Numbers

General Rule. In general, the following are spelled out: whole numbers from one through one hundred, round numbers, and any number beginning a sentence. Numerals are used for other numbers.

Numbers

> The College plans to add 112 new employees within the next five years.
>
> Seventy people were killed during the most recent hurricane.

Round Numbers. Whether used exactly or as approximations, round numbers such as hundreds, thousands, hundred thousands, and millions are spelled out (except in the sciences).

> Approximately seventy million people watched the last presidential debate.

Physical Quantities

Physical Quantities

Whole Numbers plus Fractions. Quantities that consist of both a whole number and a fraction may be spelled out when short in length. However, sometimes it is better to express the number and fraction in numerals.

> The race was a total of six and three-quarter miles.
>
> Barb required 3½ skeins of yarn to complete the scarf.

Abbreviations and Symbols. When using an abbreviation for a unit of measure, the quantity is expressed as a numeral.

> My vehicle averages 28 miles per gallon during a highway road trip.

Percentages

Percentages. Percentages are given in numerals.

> Only 16 percent of the candidates qualified for the position.

Dates

The Year Alone. Unless a year begins a sentence (which should generally be avoided), it is expressed in numerals.

> The 2008 presidential election has created an extreme amount of concern for voters.

The Day of the Month. Numerals are used when expressing dates. When a day without a month is listed, the number is spelled out.

> October 8, 2008, was a rainy day.
>
> We will have volunteers work on the sixteenth this month.

Centuries. Centuries are spelled out and lowercased.

> the twentieth century

Time of Day

Spelled-out Forms. Even, half, and quarter hours of time are spelled out in text. When using *o'clock*, the number is also spelled out.

> School ends at one-thirty in the afternoon.
>
> Monday I need to get up at five o'clock.

Numerals. When citing exact times, numerals are used (with zeros for even hours). If using a.m. or p.m., use lowercase lettering with a period following each letter (do not space after the period).

> Roberta will arrive at her destination on the 4:46 p.m. train.
>
> The plane departs Pensacola at 9:12 a.m. and arrives in Detroit at 1:36 p.m.

Noon and Midnight. Do not use numerals to express noon or midnight.

> The union meeting continued well after midnight.

Names

Titles of Works. To designate the sequel to a novel or movie, roman numerals are utilized.

> *Toy Story II*

Military and Judicial Divisions. Ordinal numbers of one hundred or less relating to political or judicial divisions are spelled out.

Judicial Divisions.

> Eighth Precinct   Fourteenth District Court

Places of Worship. Ordinal numbers that are part of the official name of worship are spelled out.

> Third Presbyterian Church

Plurals and Punctuation of Numbers

Plurals. Numbers in their plural form are spelled out. Numerals form their plural by adding *s* (no apostrophe is required).

> The middle-aged workers were in their thirties.
>
> The 1950s were my favorite years.

Comma between Digits. Commas are used between groups of three digits, counting from the right, in numerals of one thousand or more. However, no commas are used in page numbers, addresses, and years.

Plurals and Punctuation of Numbers

6,942	47,727	49,968,125

The University is located at 1500 University Drive.

Inclusive Numbers

When to Use the En Dash (–). The en dash (as wide as a capital *N*) is used between two numbers that imply *up to and including* or *through*.

Inclusive Numbers

The assignment will cover pages 97–121.

When Not to Use the En Dash (–). The en dash should not be used if the word *from* or *between* is placed before the first of two numbers. Instead, *from* should be followed by *through* or *to*.

from 1987 to 1995	from April through July

Abbreviations
General Comments

Use abbreviations sparingly in text, as they can display informal or very technical writing.

Periods. Use periods with abbreviations that are written in lowercase letters. However, do not use periods with abbreviations that appear in full capitals or small capitals (regardless of the amount of letters utilized). Additionally, some exceptions may occur. One such exception is *U.S.*

Abbreviations: General Comments

Spacing or No Spacing between Elements. Regardless of lowercase or uppercase, do not leave a space between the letters of initialisms and acronyms.

Upper versus Lowercase. Noun forms are generally uppercase; adverbial forms are generally lowercase.

Ampersands (&). When used with an initialism, no space is left on either side of an ampersand.

Names and Titles

Personal Names. Generally speaking, abbreviations are not used for given names. However, a signature can be transcribed as the person wrote it. Once the person's full name is used in the text, use just the surname in subsequent references.

Initials in Personal Names. A period and a space are placed after initials representing a given name. Even if the middle initial does not stand for a name, a period is generally utilized.

P. K. Kennedy	J. R. Reynolds

Titles before Names. Civil or military titles that precede a full name can be abbreviated. However, if preceding a surname alone, the title is spelled out.

Rep. Roberta Gilbertson	Senator Hubert

Abbreviations: Names and Titles

Social Titles. Regardless of whether the title precedes the full name or the surname only, always abbreviate.

Mr.	Mrs.	Ms.	Dr.

Reverend/Honorable. When using *the, Reverend* and *Honorable* are spelled out. However, use the abbreviations *Rev.* and *Hon.* when no *the* precedes the title.

Rev. Lynne M. Moody	the Honorable Ralph E. Weibel

Jr., Sr., and the Like. Abbreviations such as *Jr.* as well as roman or arabic numerals such as *III* or *3rd* after a person's name are part of the individual's name. As such, they are retained with any given title. Only use abbreviations when the full name is provided, not just the surname.

Mr. John S. Ahern Sr.	Dr. Daniel Stone III

Academic Degrees. Unless needed for tradition or consistency, omit periods included with academic degrees. However, when following an individual's name, some professional, religious, and other designations are set off by commas.

Sandra W. Valensky, PhD	Michael Smith, DDS

Commonly used Generic Abbreviations. Some commonly used generic abbreviations include the following:

| Assoc. | Bros. | Corp. | Ltd. | Mfg. |

Company Names. In notes, bibliographies, tabular matter, etc., abbreviations and ampersands for company names are acceptable.

Agencies and Organizations

Associations and the Like. Abbreviations that are either acronyms or initialisms appear in full capitals and without periods.

Broadcasting Companies. No periods are used after call letters of radio stations and television channels.

| CBS | NATO | PBS |

Saints. When space is limited, do not spell out the word *Saint* before the name of a Christian saint. Instead, the abbreviation *St.* should be utilized. However, if ample space is available, the entire word *(Saint)* may be spelled out.

Geographical Terms

U.S. States. The two-letter (no-period) state abbreviation should be used when following the name of a city in a citation. In tables, figures, citations, and mailing addresses, abbreviate the names of U.S. states using the two-letter, no-period postal codes created by the U.S. Postal Service.

| Cleveland, OH | Boston, MA |

Canadian Provinces and Territories. Canadian provinces and territories can be abbreviated in bibliographies, but they should be spelled out in text.

Names of Countries

When to Abbreviate. Country names are spelled out. However, they may be abbreviated in tabular matter, lists, and the like.

U.S. or US. U.S. typically appears with periods; however, periods may be omitted. *United States* used as a noun should be spelled out; when used as an adjective, it can be abbreviated.

Designations of Time

Time of the Day. If using small capitals, no periods are necessary. Typically the following abbreviations are utilized:

a.m.	p.m.

Days and Months. In text, spell out and capitalize the names of days of the week and the months of the year. When using tables, figures, and citations, abbreviations can be used as long as they are consistently utilized.

Tuesday	March	December

Quotations

Run-In or Set-Off Explained. Quotations can be either run in (integrated into the text in the same type size as the text and placed in quotation marks) or set off from the text as block quotations. Block quotations are not placed in quotation marks and begin with a new line.

In general, length determines whether to use the run in or block. A short quotation, less than five lines, is run in. One hundred words or more, or at least five lines, are set off as a block quotation.

Initial Capital or Lowercase Letter

Capital to Lowercase Initial Letter: Run-in Quotations. Capitalize the first word in a direct quotation. Do not capitalize the first word of a direct quotation when it is blended into the main sentence.

The instructor noted, "Multiple revisions will be necessary."
The instructor firmly believes that "multiple revisions" will be necessary.

Introductory Phrases and Punctuation

Use of the Colon. Formal introductory phrases are followed by a colon.

Employees are motivated by two factors: praise and financial reward.

Use of the Comma. When leading into a direct quotation, a comma is used after verbs such as *said, asked*, etc.

> Mr. Moore noted, "Children are the lifeblood of the world."

Paragraphs

Paragraph Indention. Block quotations should reflect the original paragraphing.

Text Following a Block Quotation. If the wording following a block quotation is a continuation of the paragraph that introduced the actual quotation, it begins flush left. If, however, the text following the block quotation starts a new paragraph, a paragraph indentation is necessary.

Quotation Marks

Quotations and "Quotations within Quotations." Quoted words, phrases, or sentences are placed in double quotation marks. When using quotations within quotations, use single quotation marks.

> Dr. Robertson has been noted for saying, "This is 'premier' evidence."

Placement of Closing Quotation Marks. Periods, question marks, and exclamation points are placed within the set of quotation marks when the actual quotation is a complete sentence.

> Dr. Connie Harrison stated, "It's all in how you choose to look at it!"

Ellipses

The Three Dot Method Explained. Most general and many scholarly works use the three-dot method. No more than three spaced periods are used, regardless of where the omission occurs.

> Questions that define an academic institution's culture include many . . . how outsiders describe the institution . . . whether politics exist within the institution . . . what is the hierarchy of command?

The Three-or-Four Dot Method Explained. Poetry and most scholarly works use the three-or-four dot method. Three dots imply that one or more words were omitted within the sentence. Four dots indicate that one or more sentences were omitted.

If using three dots, a space occurs both before and after each period. When using four dots, however, the first dot is the actual period. As such, there is no space before the first period.

> Achieving diversity . . . does not require quotas.
>
> People are comfortable knowing that a college education is imperative. . . . If education were not financially viable, . . .

Quotations:
Ellipses

The Three-or-Four Dot Method with other Punctuation. A comma, a colon, a semicolon, a question mark, or an exclamation point may be placed before or after three ellipsis points. However, they are never used with four ellipsis points.

> As a result, . . . schools have experienced declines in minority populations.

Deliberately Incomplete Sentence. Three dots are placed at the end of an intentionally grammatically incomplete sentence.

> The majority of the *Star Spangled Banner* is known by most people, "Oh, say, can you see, by the dawn's early . . ." But how many individuals know the entire lyrics?

Whole or Partial Paragraphs Omitted. Omitting one or more paragraphs within a quotation is indicated by four ellipsis marks at the end of the paragraph prior to the omitted portion. However, if the paragraph ends with an incomplete sentence, only three ellipsis marks are required.

> A college education now has the status that a high school education had a decade or so ago. . . . The public now realizes that education helps boost the economy.

Sections and Subheadings

Sections and Subheadings

- Long chapters in theses and dissertations and long class papers may need to be divided into sections for easier reading.
- When subheadings are used, use at least two levels; two or three levels are sufficient unless writing a long, complex paper.

- A blank line should be inserted both above and below each subhead.

- Some universities may have a format for using various subheadings. If not, one needs to be devised and consistently followed throughout the paper. One such format is as follows:

First Level: centered, headline style capitalization, italicized

Second Level: centered, headline style capitalization, roman type

Third Level: flush left, headline style capitalization, italicized

Fourth Level: flush left, headline style capitalization, italicized

Fifth Level: run-in at start of sentence, sentence style capitalization, italicized, period at end

Citing Sources in Text

Full Source Given. A source in its entirety can be given in parentheses immediately following a quotation. Or, part of the data may be inserted into the text, with specific details placed in parentheses.

> (Robert K. Yin, *Case Study Research: Design and Methods* [Thousand Oaks: SAGE Publications, 2003], 83).
>
> As stated in Yin's *Case Study Research: Design and Methods* (SAGE Publications, 2003), the design of a study is extremely important.

Ibid. The term *ibid* (set in roman) may be used in place of other bibliographic information in a second parenthetical reference if the passage is from the same source and is quoted closely to the first. This is only allowed if there are no intervening quotations from other sources. It should be followed by a period, a comma, and the page number of the source.

> (Ibid., 231)

Sources Following Run-in Quotations

No Period Preceding Source. Cite the source after the closing quotation mark of a run-in quotation, and follow with the remaining words or punctuation of the sentence.

Quotations:
Sources Following Run-In Quotations

> Dr. Smith noted, "College attendance can increase financial records" (*Leadership*, 176).

Question Mark or Exclamation Point. A quotation placed at the end of a sentence that is itself a question or exclamation requires the punctuation to come before the closing quotation mark. The final period is added *after* the closing parenthesis.

> "What type of leader are you?" (Sayers, 142).

Sources Following Block Quotations

Placement and Punctuation. The source of a block quotation is typed in the same font size and is placed in parentheses at the end of the quotation. The first parenthesis is typed after the final punctuation mark of the quotation. There are no periods either before or after the final parenthesis.

Quotations:
Sources Following Block Quotations

> (Robert K. Yin, *Case Study Research: Design and Methods* [Thousand Oaks: SAGE Publications, 2003], 83)

Illustrations

Placement and Numbering

Placement. Illustrations should appear as soon as possible after the initial text reference in printed works. They may, however, be placed after the reference if they appear on the same page or same two-page spread as the reference or if the text does not allow appropriate space to list all figures and tables after their respective references.

Illustrations:
Placement and Numbering

When illustrations are dispersed throughout the entire document, it must be indicated in the manuscript approximately where each is to be located (use *see 6.8*) (in roman).

Numerals and Letters. Use arabic numerals for all illustrations. Do not capitalize the word *figure* in text references to figures. Also do not abbreviate *figure* as *fig.* except in parenthetical references.

(see fig. 13)	(see fig. 11.2c)

Captions

Syntax, Punctuation, and Capitalization. A caption may consist of a few words, an incomplete sentence, a complete sentence, several sentences, or a combination. If a caption is an incomplete sentence, no punctuation is needed. If one or multiple complete sentences follow an incomplete caption, each sentence has the appropriate closing punctuation.

Harvard University graduation ceremony, 2008

Formal Titles. Generally speaking, titles of most works of art are capitalized in headline style and italicized, whether alone or incorporated into a caption.

Auguste Rodin, *The Thinker*

Caption with Number. Illustration numbers can be separated from the caption by a period. If the number is typographically distinct, it may be separated by a space.

Figure 5. Adult issues

Identifying Placement. If a caption does not fit on the same page as the illustration, use explanatory wording (placed in italics if needed). The caption should appear at the foot or head of the closest text page.

Opposite: Percentage of malaria cases

Identifying a Figure with Several Parts. Identify the parts in the caption with terms such as *left, right, top, bottom, left to right, clockwise*, etc. The term is italicized and followed by a comma.

Figure 3. *Above left*, Dr. Robert Williams; *above right*, Dr. Henry Birch; *below left*, Dr. Susan Tienken; *below right*, Dr. Jane Letica

Source Lines

Source. A source line, otherwise known as a short statement of the source of an illustration, is generally appropriate and sometimes required. Illustrations created by the author are an exception. A phrase such as *Photo by author* is appropriate.

Permissions. Whether published or unpublished, material under copyright generally requires permission from the copyright owner.

Placement. Source lines generally appear at the end of a caption. They are placed in parentheses or in different type. A photographer's name will sometimes be placed in small type located parallel to the bottom or side of a photograph.

Form. The language, or form, of a source line is dependent on its placement and the type and copyright status of the illustration. Source lines generally follow a consistent pattern within a work.

Illustrations:
Source Lines

Author's Own Material. Illustrations created by the author do not require source lines. However, a phrase such as *Photo by author* is appropriate if other illustrations in the same work require credit.

Material Obtained Free of Charge. The term *courtesy* may be used for material that has been obtained free of charge and without use restrictions.

Material Requiring Permission. An illustration reproduced from a published work under copyright protection requires formal permission, unless fair use applies. The source line should include a page or figure number, along with the author, title, publication details, and (if available) copyright date.

Material in the Public Domain. While a source line is appropriate, illustrations from works in the public domain may be reproduced without permission.

Adapted Material. If an author uses data from another source or adjusts the data from another source, credit for the originating source should be given.

Charts

Essential Properties. A chart should be used only if it summarizes the data more appropriately than written words. The chart should be displayed in a relatively simple and comprehensible graphic form.

Consistency. Charts must abide by a consistent style in both graphics and typography when two or more are utilized within a particular work.

Illustrations:
Charts

Graphs: The Axes. Both the *x* (horizontal) and *y* (vertical) axes must be appropriately labeled. The *y* axis label is read from the bottom up.

Graphs: The Curves. Curves should be presented in graphically distinct forms, such as a continuous line, broken line, etc. All elements should be identified in a caption or in a key.

Labels in Relation to Captions. The title of a chart is identified in the caption below the chart in printed works.

Abbreviations. Abbreviations and symbols are allowed in labels provided that they are recognizable or described in a key or in the caption.

Main Parts of a Table (See table example at the end of this section)

Table Number

Form. All tables are given an arabic numeral and should be cited directly or parenthetically in the text by the number.

Tables:
Number

Tabular Matter not Requiring a Number. A short list requiring only two columns does not need to be numbered or titled.

Number Sequence. Table numbers follow the order in which the actual tables are placed in the text.

Table Title

Length. The title of a table should briefly identify the contents of the table.

Tables:
Title

Syntax. The title should be developed in noun form.

Capitalization. Table titles are capitalized in sentence format.

Parenthetical Information. Significant explanatory or statistical information can be included in parentheses within the title.

Number plus Title. The number of a table should precede the title of the table. Both number and title should appear on the same line.

Column Heads

Treatment. Column heads (horizontal axis) should be brief and developed in sentence format.

Explanatory Tags. An explanatory tag or subheading is sometimes included in the column head. The tag, either a symbol or abbreviation, is placed in parentheses.

Numbered Columns. When columns require numbers for text reference, arabic numerals should be placed in parentheses. The number and parentheses should be centered immediately below the column head and above the line separating the head from the actual column.

The Stub

Definition. The stub is the left-hand column of a table (vertical axis). It is generally a vertical list of categories that are further explained in the respective table columns.

Stub Entries and Subentries. Items in the stub may be a sequential or classified list. If a subentry is required (just like with a main entry), the first word is capitalized. This capitalization will avoid confusion that might result with runover lines.

Typographic Treatment of Subentries. Subentries must be clearly identified from main entries and runover lines. Subentries may be indented. Alternatively, italics may be used for the main entries while roman should be used for the subentries.

Runover Lines. When no subentries are utilized, runover lines are indented one em. Runovers can be placed flush left if there is extra space between rows.

Abbreviations and the Like. If space is limited, symbols or abbreviations are acceptable in the stub portion of the table. However, ditto marks are not permissible.

Totals. Indent the word *total* if used at the end of a stub. It can be indented deeper than the greatest indentation found within the table, or it may be distinguished typographically.

The Body and the Cells

Table Body. The body of a table is comprised of information in columns to the right of the stub and below the column heading. Cells are spaces within columns. Generally, the cells contain data; however, they sometimes are empty.

Column Data. All data in individual columns should hold the same types of information. For example, dollar values might be in one column and percentages in another column.

Empty Cells. If a column head is not applicable to one of the stub entries, the cell may be left blank, filled in with an em dash, or filled in with three unspaced ellipses dots.

Horizontal Alignment. Cells align horizontally to respective stub entries.

Vertical Alignment: With Column Head. Column heads are centered on the longest cell entry. However, the stub head and all stub entries are aligned to the left.

Vertical Alignment: Numerals. Columns comprised of numerals without commas or decimal points are aligned on the last number.

Vertical Alignment: Words. When columns are comprised of words, phrases, or sentences, visual appearance determines vertical alignment. If there are no runover lines, entries may be centered. If entries are long, they may begin flush left.

Zeros before Decimal Points. Zeros are generally added before the decimal point with numbers less than 1.00. In tables, however, they may be omitted if preferred.

Totals, Averages, Means: Typographic Treatment. Additional vertical space or short lines periodically appear above totals at the end of columns. However, they are not required. No lines should appear above averages or means.

When to Use Totals. Totals and subtotals may or may not be included in the table. If useful to the presentation of the data, they may be desirable.

Signs and Symbols. In columns exclusively consisting of signs or symbols, the signs or symbols are omitted from the individual cells and included in the column head.

<table>
<tr><td colspan="5">Table 6.1 Sample First-year Program of Study</td></tr>
<tr><td>Quarter Taken[1]</td><td>Seminar Number</td><td>Seminar Title</td><td>Credits</td><td>Grade[2] Received</td></tr>
<tr><td colspan="5">Year 1</td></tr>
<tr><td rowspan="2">Quarter 1</td><td>BUS 800</td><td>Doctoral Seminar in Information Proficiency</td><td>2</td><td></td></tr>
<tr><td>BUS 801</td><td>The Scholar Practitioner</td><td>4</td><td></td></tr>
<tr><td rowspan="2">Quarter 2</td><td>BUS 810</td><td>Leading 21st Century Organizations</td><td>4</td><td></td></tr>
<tr><td>BUS 890</td><td>Portfolio Development I</td><td>2</td><td></td></tr>
<tr><td rowspan="2">Quarter 3</td><td>BUS 813</td><td>Quality and Organizational Change</td><td>4</td><td></td></tr>
<tr><td>BUS 891</td><td>Portfolio Development II</td><td>2</td><td></td></tr>
<tr><td rowspan="2">Quarter 4</td><td>BUS 811</td><td>Managing in a World-Wide Context</td><td>4</td><td></td></tr>
<tr><td>BUS 892</td><td>Comprehensive Essay</td><td>2</td><td></td></tr>
<tr><td>During Yr 1</td><td>BUS 880</td><td>Professional Residency</td><td>2</td><td></td></tr>
<tr><td colspan="5">[1] Enter the actual/planned quarter taken. For example, Spring 2008.
[2] Enter your grade upon completion of the seminar.</td></tr>
</table>

Tables

Part Four:
Source Citation

All researchers need to properly cite the ideas, words, or findings of others in their work. This is done to give proper credit to those deserving it, assure readers of information accuracy, and aid readers in following and expanding upon the research.

Essentially, source citations should be included when exact words are quoted from a source, information is paraphrased, or ideas are used. Citation styles differ (APA, MLA, CMS, etc.) but the goal is to supply the reader with enough information to locate sources utilized in text. This information should include all or some of the following:

- Important people – author, editor, director, producer, or translator.

- Book, journal, recording, database, chapter, article, collection, series, volume, edition, page numbers, URL, or any other locating information that is specific to that particular work.

- Publisher, publication date, publication place or a note that the document has not been published if this is the case.

Citation Styles

The two basic documentation systems for citing sources are the (1) *notes and bibliography* system and (2) *author-date* system. The goal of either system is to give credit to deserving authors and allow readers to locate published or unpublished material utilized within the writing. Both systems are discussed for clarification and understanding.

The *notes and bibliography* system (humanities style) is used by writers in the arts, history, and literature. Information that is paraphrased, summarized, or quoted is cited by footnotes or endnotes (listing the author, title, and facts of publication) that are typically supplemented with a bibliography. Footnotes are placed in-text at the bottom or foot of the page where the citation occurs. Endnotes are placed collectively at the end of the paper. Footnotes and endnotes are designated with a raised arabic numeral that immediately follows the work being recognized (the numerals are full sized, not raised, in the notes themselves), and these numerals are listed in consecutive order, beginning with 1, throughout the paper. If endnotes and footnotes are both used in the same document, endnotes are referenced with numbers and footnotes are referenced with symbols (asterisks, daggers, parallels, etc.). Footnotes and endnotes referring to tables or other non-textual matter are numbered independently (using letters) from those referring to textual matter.

Citation Styles

The *bibliography* provides an overview of utilized sources and lists works cited on a separate page. In the rare instance that there is no bibliography or the bibliography contains only a selected list, then full details (including page number) are given in the footnotes or endnotes at first mention of any work cited. Footnotes and endnotes are concise if the bibliography contains complete details of all works in order to avoid duplication of information. This system is excellent for a diverse assortment of sources, including those that are obscure or inappropriate for the author-date system.

The *author-date* system is used by writers in the natural, physical, and social sciences. Paraphrased, summarized, or quoted sources are cited in text, typically in parentheses, using the author's surname, publication date, and page numbers. Complete details of the sources are listed in the *reference list*. Parenthetical citations (listing authors, publication dates, page numbers, volume numbers, sections, and comments) are also used in text to direct readers to the reference list for full details. When authors' names appear in text, they need not be repeated in parenthetical citation. This system works best when sources can be easily converted to author-date citations. Other sources, such as manuscripts and anonymous works, are typically better referred to in footnotes and endnotes.

Both source documentation systems can be combined if necessary. For example, a paper utilizing mostly footnotes and endnotes can include some parenthetical citations in text, and a paper following the author-date methodology can contain some notes. Students unsure of citation style requirements for writing a paper, thesis, or dissertation should consult with their instructors or advisors.

Electronic Sources (Internet)

Researchers are increasingly using sources found online or in some other electronic medium. However, concerns remain about this type of information. Consider the following:

- Electronic sources are not as stable as print sources due to their ability to change content or location at any given time. The changes are sometimes made without revision dates, making it difficult to verify the accuracy of the information. Additionally, there are currently no official standards for establishing the definition of a revision, so a revision date might signify something as simple as a correction of a grammatical error or something as critical as update of new research findings.

- Electronic sources do not always list authors, editors, or publishers. Those sources are considered anonymous and might be questionable as reliable sources of information.

- URLs (uniform resource locators) are not always available as time passes. This creates hardship for readers attempting to find the original content.

Students should ask instructors or advisors about what types of online sources are acceptable for use. This helps prevent problems after the document has been written.

For online sources such as journals, books, newspapers, and magazines, include the URL and access date (examples are included in this book) in addition to publication information that would be listed if the source were in print. For online sources such as web sites and electronic mailing lists, give locator or identifier information in addition to the URL and access date (examples are included in this book). Online databases and periodicals" that are subscription based do not need to be listed as "subscription-based" or "restricted."

CD-ROMs tend to be more stable sources than those found online. When using CD-ROMs, the medium should be listed in addition to publication information (examples are included in this book).

Citation Preparation

- If multiple versions for a source are available, cite the actual version used.

- Record bibliographical information immediately so this is not forgotten after note taking.

- List page numbers for direct quotations and paraphrasing.

- Place citations in the draft document to help remember where they go after the document is written.

- Review citations for accuracy while the document is in the draft form.

- Check carefully for errors in bibliography or reference section entries.

- Use caution when using a software program designed to automatically insert citations (footnotes, endnotes, bibliographies, or reference lists) because these are not always accurate.

Notes and Bibliography System
Footnotes

- Footnotes are sometimes preferred over endnotes because all pertinent information is available on the same page.

- Readers of scholarly work often prefer footnotes to endnotes due to ease of reference.

- A superscripted arabic numeral in text represents a word, sentence, phrase, or quote.

- The superscripted arabic numeral in text should appear as close as possible to the word, sentence, phrase, or quote that it represents, but it is sometimes best to place it at the end of the sentence to minimize confusion.

Acceptable
Ariel Roddy's most recent book, *Campus Encounters: Life as a Soccer Player at Amherst College,*[1] was published over five years ago.

Preferable
Ariel Roddy's most recent book, *Campus Encounters: Life as a Soccer Player at Amherst College,* was published over five years ago.[1]

- The superscripted numbers in text run consecutively throughout the document or start new with each chapter.

- There is no space between the superscripted arabic numeral in text and the word, sentence, phrase, or quote.

- If citing several sources to support a single point, group them all into one footnote in order to avoid a cluttered look. Separate each entry with a semi-colon.

Drinking in establishments other than those legally authorized for such a purpose can result in problems with the police. Alcohol cannot be sold to the public unless a license is obtained and hours or operation meet state or federal requirements.[2]

---

2. Jessica Pottsburg, "Illegal Drinking," *Police Review* 21 (2009): 2-9; Paige Mendleworth, "Power and Policy," *Government Politics* 14 (2008): 121-35; Benjamin Crantle, *Local Police and National Policy* (Pueblo, CO: Harter Mills, 2009).

- Place corresponding entries at the foot (or bottom) of the page where the source is referenced in text. Place a short line between the last line of text and the first footnote.

- Entries at the bottom of a page must correspond with reference numbers in text.

- If text runs short on a page (such as at the end of a chapter), still place the entry at the bottom of the page.

- If an entry is too long for one page, it should be completed at the bottom of the next page. However, all footnotes should at least begin on the page on which they are referenced.

- Indent the first line of each entry at the bottom of the page as you would a paragraph. The following lines are flush with the left margin.

Footnotes

- Single space each entry at the bottom of the page, and double space between entries.

- A *footnote* feature is available on many word processing programs (such as Microsoft Word).

Publicly berating a subordinate in order to achieve positive behavioral change is often accepted in the military.[1] A boot camp drill sergeant, for example, may scream at a new recruit and call him or her derogatory names because his or her bed was not made properly. This type of verbal abuse would probably not be accepted if a hotel manager were to reprimand a maid in a similar manner for the same infraction.[2]

---

1. Peeka T. Tonto, *Military Systems* (Chicago: Rottweiler Books, 2009), 131.

2. Harold Barnsworth, *Resort & Hotel Etiquette: Training for Employees* (London: Pankin Books, 2009), 21-28.

Endnotes

- Endnotes are sometimes preferred over footnotes because they leave pages looking less cluttered.

- Tables, quoted poetry, and similar matter are preferably listed in endnotes instead of footnotes.

- A superscripted arabic numeral in text represents a word, sentence, phrase, or quote.

- The superscripted arabic numeral in text should appear as close as possible to the word, sentence, phrase, or quote that it represents, but it is sometimes best to place it at the end of the sentence to minimize confusion. See the *footnote* section for an example.

- The superscripted numbers in text run consecutively throughout the document or start new with each chapter.

- There is no space between the superscripted arabic numeral in text and the word, sentence, phrase, or quotation.

- Place corresponding entries on a separate *notes* page at the end of a document or end of a chapter.

- Entries on the notes page must correspond with reference numbers in text.

- The notes page contains the heading *Notes*, which is centered at the top of the page.

- Double space between the heading and the first entry on the notes page.

- Indent the first line of each entry on the notes page as you would a paragraph. The following lines are flush with left margin.

- Single space each entry on the notes page, and double space between entries.

- An *endnote* feature is available on many word processing programs (such as Microsoft Word).

In General (Footnotes and Endnotes)

Footnotes and Endnotes

- List as they occur (not alphabetically like *bibliographies* and *reference lists*).

- Authors (editors, compilers, or translators) are listed as they appear on the sources (in the first reference; in subsequent references, list only the surname).

- Authors' (editors', compilers', or translators') given names are used instead of initials if known, unless those individuals prefer initials (in the first reference; in subsequent references, list only the surname).

- Titles of work appear in full in the first reference and are shortened in subsequent references (using key words) if the titles contain more than four words. Shortened titles contain key words from full titles and wording order is not changed.

- Publication dates appear after the publishers (in the first reference only).

- Page numbers are not listed if the work is being referred to as a whole.

- Page numbers are not listed for books unless citing specific chapters or passages.

- Beginning and ending page numbers of articles are listed

for journals when referencing the article as a whole. When referring to a specific passage, only those page numbers are listed.

- Page numbers are listed for electronic sources (if available).

- Electronic sources list pages, sections, equations, or other divisions of work if available. If not available (which is often the case), list nothing.

Titles of books and names of journals are italicized.

- Titles of articles, chapters, and poems are placed in quotation marks.

- Titles of books, articles, and journal names are capitalized headline style (lower and uppercase lettering).

- Paragraph indents (within the same footnote or endnote) are avoided to prevent confusion.

- Footnotes and endnotes may contain citations plus commentary; however, complicated information (lists, tabular material, etc.) is placed in the appendix section.

- If more than ten abbreviations of titles, names, manuscript collections, etc. are used, then they are listed along with the unabbreviated form in alphabetical order in a separate section headed *Abbreviations*.

- If there are two or three authors, all are listed in the first and subsequent references.

- If there are more than three authors, list all of them in the first reference, then list the first author followed by *et al.* in subsequent references.

Footnotes and Endnotes

1 through 4 are examples of cited sources, and 5 through 8 are examples of shortened forms of subsequent citations for the same sources:

1. Peter N. Steriata, *Wealth in China: Benefits of Industrialization* (Boston: Paramount, 2009).

2. Malcolm N. Taliholm, "Management Perspectives on TQM in Automotive Manufacturing," *Quality Review* 13, no. 4 (2009): 124-38.

3. Pierre Boggles, *France's Dark Side: Real World Stories of a Made Man,* ed. P. L. Marles (New York: New York University Press, 2008).

4. Parker M Findlay, Richard Pebbles, David Promes, and F. M. Dannit, "Teen Related Gang Deaths: Research in Urban Cleveland," *Journal of Youth Behavior* 10, no. 3 (2008): 104-18.

5. Steriata, *Wealth in China.*

6. Taliholm, "Management Perspectives," 125, 129.

7. Boggles, *France's Dark Side*, 109.

8. Findlay et al., "Teen Related Gang Deaths," 107.

Footnotes and Endnotes

- The word *ibid.* refers to the immediately preceding endnote or footnote by taking the place of all the required information.

- List a page number if different than the immediately preceding endnote or footnote page number.

3. Campbell, *Thinking Positive*, 214.

4. Ibid., 112-113.

- Quotations are in quotation marks followed by the source.

1. Patel notes: "The touch screen is made for wet processing areas." Maria K. Millworth, *Computer Programming* (Cincinnati: Cincinnati College Press, 2009), 152.

- Footnotes continuing on another page must break in mid-sentence to avoid missing the end of the note.

> *Bottom of page 12*
> 16. Bigglesdorf stated the following during her diagnosis: "We don't always know why things happen, but we can often make reasonable guesses based on the psychological
>
> *Next page*
> and physiological information available to us," Arnola Gallion, *Modern Science* (Memphis: University of Memphis Press, 2009), 211.

- Endnotes for a book are placed together, after the text and appendixes and before the bibliography. The main heading is *Notes*, and the notes for each chapter are introduced with that chapter as a subheading. However, if a book has different authors for each chapter, then the endnotes are placed at the end of each chapter under a *Notes* heading.

> *(Assume the text portion of the document ends here)*
>
> Chapter One
>
> 1. War signaled a need for change, and that is why the ruling monarchy made decisions that were questionable at the time. See Mildred Gainsworth, *Fateful Decisions of English Rulers* (Chicago: Mylander, 2009), 188.
>
> 2. Fransen stated: "London had its own share of problems during that revolutionary period." Mitch Vessler, *European History* (Baltimore: University of Baltimore Press, 2009), 135.
>
> Chapter Two
>
> 1. Tyrus D. Charmel noted: "The conservative tradition must be upheld under the worst of circumstances." Jerome Mills, *Monarchies* (Las Vegas: University of Nevada Press, 2009), 14.

Footnotes and Endnotes

- Endnotes in journals are placed at the end of each article under a *Notes* heading.

Parenthetical Notes

- When the reader sees many references to a few sources, these sources can be cited in text within parentheses instead of using footnotes or endnotes. Examples include newspaper articles and biblical or sacred works.

- Place the citation where a reference number for a note would normally be placed in text.

- A full citation is typically provided in the bibliography.

Parenthetical note

According to one athlete, the situation worsened when steroids became a normal occurrence in locker rooms across the United States (Freckles, "Natural Healing," 148).

Bibliography

Freckles, James R. "Natural Healing." *Journal of Sports Medicine* 21 (2009): 146-54.

Bibliographies

- This section is similar, but not identical, to the *Reference* or *Works Cited* section in the *author-date* system.

- Bibliographies are used with footnotes or endnotes.

- Full bibliographies include all cited works (books, articles, and other references). The heading of a full bibliography is *Bibliography*.

- Selected bibliographies contain only the most important works cited and contain a head note explaining the reasoning for selection. The heading of a selected bibliography is *Selected Bibliography*.

- Single-author bibliographies list works by one person, and these are typically listed as an addition to the standard bibliography. The heading of this section is *Works of [Author's Name], Writings of [Author's name],* or something similar. Single-author bibliography entries are often arranged chronologically, instead of alphabetically, because this is more useful to the reader.

- Annotated bibliographies annotate each entry with a short description of the work relevance or content. Brief annotation phrases are placed in brackets after the publication data (using no periods). The heading of this section is *Annotated Bibliography.*

- Single space individual bibliography entries and double space between each entry.

- Entries use the hanging indent feature. The first line of each entry is flush left, and the following lines are indented.

- References are listed in alphabetical order by authors (using surname of first author), associations (if the work is authored by an organization), or place or thing (if work is anonymous).

- Authors are listed by surnames. If no author is provided, the entries are alphabetized according to the first word of the title (ignore *A, An,* or *The*).

- Multiple author entries invert the first author's name and list subsequent authors as written.

Bently, Jackson James, Marie Altec, Andrea M. Jameson, and Marlene Thompson. "Living Dinosaurs: Wall Street's Last Hurrah." *Business Review* 23 (2009): 311-18.

- Multiple authors with the same surname are listed alphabetically by first name.

> Smith, Arnold. "The Fate of the Archdiocese: A Qualitative Analysis." *Religious Quarterly* 21 (2009): 12-19.
>
> Smith, Martin. *Walking with Giants*. New York: Doubleday, 2008.
>
> Smith, N. D. "Happiness of the Soul." In *Survival of the Fittest: A Historical Perspective*, edited by Gregory Porter, 291-312. Chicago: University of Chicago Press, 2009.

- Successive entries by authors with different co-authors are listed alphabetically by the first author's surname, and further alphabetized by subsequent authors.

Bibliographies

> Baker, Riley. *Professional Football: The Formative Years*. 2nd ed. Chicago: Rand McNally, 2007.
>
> Baker, Riley, and Herbert L. Fitzgerald. *Professional Football: Game Changes*. Chicago: Rand McNally, 2009.
>
> Baker, Riley, Randall Lesmark, and Anthony Tompkins. *Professional Football: America's Favorite Pastime*. Chicago: Rand McNally, 2008.

- Successive entries by the same author, editor, compiler, translator, institution, or corporate author use a 3-em dash to replace the author, editor, compiler, translator, institution, or corporate author after the first listing. The 3-em dash is followed by a period or comma, as was listed in the previous entry. Titles are listed alphabetically (ignore *A, An,* or *The*).

> *Authors*
>
> Sanders, Charles R., Michael G. Barrells, and T. M. Paulson. *Basics of Auto Racing*. Los Angeles: Harles, 2008.
>
> ———. "The Stress of Racing." In *Modern Automotive Concepts*, edited by Bernard T. Brock, 291-306. Los Angeles: Harles, 2007.

Editors

Campinari, Katrina P., Joanne T. Nellies, and Kelly
  K., Sanchose, eds. *Intermediate Mathematics in
  American High Schools*. Cincinnati: University of
  Cincinnati Press, 2008.

——. *Simple Mathematics in American Middle Schools*.
  Cincinnati: University of Cincinnati Press, 2008.

Institutions

U. S. Senate Committee on Immigration. *Determining
  Legality*. 17th Cong., 2nd sess., 1921.

——. *Immigrant Responsibility*. 84th Cong., 3rd sess., 1931.

- Authors' (editors', compilers', or translators') given
  names are used instead of initials if known unless these
  individuals prefer initials.

- Author's initials used in place of a given name are listed
  before spelled-out names beginning with the same letter.

- Acronyms, abbreviations, and initialisms are listed as they
  appear, not as fully spelled out.

- Publication dates appear after the publishers.

- Page numbers are not listed for books unless citing specific
  chapters.

- Beginning and ending page numbers of articles are listed
  for journals.

- Page numbers are listed for electronic sources (if
  available).

- Numerals are spelled out.

- Titles of books and names of journals are italicized.

- Titles of articles, chapters, and poems are placed in
  quotation marks.

- Titles of books, articles, and journal names are capitalized
  headline style.

- *A, An,* or *The* (introductory words) in titles, associations, places, or organizations are omitted.

The University of Illinois	*is listed as*	University of Illinois
The Shineworth Group	*is listed as*	Shineworth Group
The Netherlands	*is listed as*	Netherlands
The Bronx	*is listed as*	Bronx

- Personal names used as names of organizations or associations are listed as written.

E. F. Hutton & Co.	*is listed as*	E. F. Hutton & Co.
T. J. Maxx	*is listed as*	T. J. Maxx
Joseph Bank Cleaners	*is listed as*	Joseph Bank Cleaners

- Names of mountains and lakes are inverted and listed under the non-generic names.

Lake Michigan	*is listed as*	Michigan, Lake
Mount Everest	*is listed as*	Everest, Mount

- Names of cities and islands beginning with topographical elements are listed as such.

Lake Placid, NY	*is listed as*	Lake Placid, NY
Mt. Pleasant, MI	*is listed as*	Mt. Pleasant, MI
Isle of Wight	*is listed as*	Isle of Wight

- Bibliographies precede the index at the end of a document. However, textbooks and multi-authored books have bibliographies at the end of each chapter.

Bibliographies

Author-Date System

Parenthetical Citations

- Parenthetical citations are used in text to direct readers to the *reference list* for full details.

- Authors, publication dates, page numbers, volume numbers, sections, and comments are listed. When authors' names appear in text, they need not be repeated in parenthetical citation.

Author and date
(Ulysses 2008) *or* Ulysses (2008)

Author, date, and page number (comma after date)
(Norman 2007, 85) *or* Norman (2007, 85)

Author, date, and volume (comma after date)
(Lee 2009, vol. 4) *or* Lee (2009, vol. 4)

Author, date, volume, and page number (comma after date, colon after volume)
(Oberman 2008, 2:312) *or* Oberman (2008, 2:312)

Author, date, volume, and section (comma after date)
(Diamo 2008, sec. 23) *or* Diamo (2008, sec. 23)

Author, date, and comment (comma after date)
(Qualen 2009, arithmetic mean used) *or* Qualen (2009, arithmetic mean used)

- Different authors with the same surname use initials to distinguish (two initials are necessary if the first initials are the same).

(N. Smithers 2008)   (R. Smithers 2008)

- Authors with two or more works in the same year are denoted by lowercase letters *a, b, c,* etc. after the date. Letters are listed in the order they fall in the document (alphabetical order does not apply). Use *and* (not *&*) to separate authors.

> (Thatcher and West 2007a)   (Thatcher and West 2007b)

- If there are more than three authors, list only the first author followed by *et al.*

> (Yzerman et al. 2008)
>
> A study by Yzerman et al. (2008) found dogs to be more aggressive than cats.

Parenthetical Citations

- Two or more references within parentheses are separated by semi-colons. These references can be listed by importance, chronological order, or alphabetical order.

> (Wangler 2009; Welch and Anonnis 2008; Cindler et al. 2006)

- There must be a reference listing for every parenthetical citation.

- Page numbers are necessary if referring to specific passages.

- Electronic sources list pages, sections, or other divisions of work if available. If not available (which is often the case), list nothing.

Reference Lists

- This section is similar, but not identical to, the *bibliographies* section in the *notes and bibliography* system. It is used with the *author-date* system.

- Alphabetizing rules follow those in the *bibliographies* section.

Reference Lists

- There must be a parenthetical citation in text for every *reference list* citation.

- Single space individual bibliography entries and double space between each entry.

Entries use the hanging indent feature. The first line of each entry is flush left, and the following lines are indented.

- Publication dates immediately follow the authors' (editors', compilers', or translators') names.

- Multiple author entries invert the first author's name and list subsequent authors as written.

- Successive entries by the same author, editor, compiler, translator, institution, or corporate author follow the rules listed in the bibliographies section (using the 3-em dash).

- Authors with two or more works in the same year are denoted by *a, b, c*, etc., after the date. The letters are designated by the order in which the citations appeared in the text; entries are alphabetized on the reference list by title.

Laurent, Tanisha Q. 2009b. *Advanced racquetball techniques: Strategies for success*. Ithaca, NY: Solo Books.

Laurent, Tanisha Q. 2009a. *Racquetball techniques for beginners*. Ithaca, NY: Solo Books.

- Authors' (editors', compilers', or translators') initials can be used instead of full names if only initials are given (this is not uncommon in the natural sciences).

- Author's initials used in place of a given name are listed before spelled-out names beginning with the same letter.

- Publication dates are placed after the authors, editors, translators, or compilers.

Duster, Pamela R., and Terrance Tiles. 2008. *Adult friendships and adult socialization*. Cambridge, MA: MIT Press.

- Page numbers are not listed for books unless citing specific chapters.

- Beginning and ending page numbers are listed for journal articles.

- Page numbers are listed for electronic sources (if available).

- Titles of books and names of journals are italicized.

- Journal names are capitalized headline style, and titles of books and articles are capitalized sentence style.

Headline style (journal)

Journal of Organizational Behavior

Sentence style (book)

Bottle rockets: The search for perfection

Reference Lists

- *Reference lists* precede the index at the end of a document. However, textbooks and multi-authored books have *reference lists* at the end of each chapter, in which case the list is subheaded *References* or *Literature Cited.*

- Journals listing months are abbreviated.

Month	Acceptable abbreviation
January	Jan.
February	Feb.

- Science journal titles are abbreviated using the *Index Medicus* (use an Internet search engine to find *Index Medicus*) or the *BIOSIS Serial Sources* (use an Internet search engine to find *BIOSIS Serial Sources*).

- Other abbreviations are as listed below.

Phrase	Acceptable abbreviation
Edited by	ed. (capitalized if following a period)
Translated by	trans. (capitalized if following a period)
University	Univ.

Coding System

The *Turabian Manual For Writers of Research Papers, Theses, and Dissertations* (7th edition) uses the following key to designate examples for the two types of source documentation systems.

Coding System

N = Footnotes or Endnotes (*notes and bibliography* system)

B = Bibliography (*notes and bibliography* system)

P = Parenthetical citation (*author-date* system)

R = Reference list (*author-date* system)

For ease of reference, the same key will be used in this book. The following are examples of how to properly cite sources (please note that in order to condense this book, all four types of sources are not included for every example).

Books

List Entries in the Following Order.

Author – list editor or institution if no author is listed

Title – also list subtitle if applicable

Editor, Compiler, or Translator – if listed in addition to the author

Edition – if it is not the first

Books

Volume – list individual number if single volume is cited and total number if referred to as a whole

Series – list volume number within series if series is numbered

Publication city – also list state if city is not well known

Publisher

Publication date

Page number(s) – if applicable

URL (for Internet or other electronic sources)

Medium (DVD, CD-ROM, etc.) – if not a book

In General

- Titles are italicized.

- Titles in bibliographies, footnotes, and endnotes are capitalized headline style, and titles in reference lists are capitalized sentence style.

- Titles in full capital letters are changed to lower and uppercase letters (following the appropriate headline or sentence style) unless they are acronyms or initialisms.

- Italicized terms within titles (such as names of bacteria in scientific research) use roman type (reverse italics).

Supporting documentation for the study of Listeria monocytogenes *in seafood*

Books

- *Ampersands* (&) in titles are changed to *and*.

- Subtitles are separated by a colon and the first letter is capitalized (both headline and sentence style).

Headline style
B: *Illegal Prescriptions: Truth in Medicine*

Sentence style
R: *Illegal prescriptions: Truth in medicine*

Publication Facts for Footnotes, Endnotes, Bibliographies, and Reference Lists

- Publication cities must include states (and provinces or countries) if the cities are not well known or can be confused with cities of the same name in different states.

Chicago	New York	Baltimore
Port Austin, MI	Reading, PA	Wooster, OH
London	Paris	Mexico City
Waterloo, ON	Sainte-Foy, QC	Alba, Italy

- Publication states are not used if they appear in the publisher names.

Brookings. South Dakota State University Press

- Unknown publication place list *n.p.* (*N.p.* if after a period) as the place of publication.

- Unknown publication dates follow same procedure as publication places, but list *n.d.* or *N.d.* as the dates of publication.

N: 1. Roneeka Watson, *Textile Giants: The Greatest American Men Ever* (n.p.: Morton, 1911).

B: Watson, Roneeka. *Textile Giants: The Greatest American Men Ever.* N.p.: Morton, 1911.

- Omit *The* from the beginning of publisher's names.

- Omit *Inc.* and *Ltd.* from publisher's names

- Retain *Books* in publisher's names,

- Retain *Press* if listed in the name of a university press or newspaper, but omit it if listed in the name of a company.

The Prudential	is listed as	Prudential
Tagon, Inc.	is listed as	Tagon
Elementary Books	is listed as	Elementary Books
Purdue University Press	is listed as	Purdue University Press
San Juan Free Press (newspaper)	is listed as	San Juan Free Press
Kellman Press (company)	is listed as	Kellman

- Publication dates list year only (not month or day).

- Use *forthcoming* for works that are in press with unknown publication dates. Use a comma between authors and *forthcoming* in parenthetical citations. Capitalize *forthcoming* in reference lists only.

N:	2. Meredith Applegate and Melody Snelling, *Absenteeism Policies in Maryland Middle Schools* (Baltimore: Paragon, forthcoming).
B:	Applegate, Meredith, and Melody Snelling. *Absenteeism Policies in Maryland Middle Schools*. Baltimore: Paragon, forthcoming.
P:	(Applegate and Snelling, forthcoming)
R:	Applegate, Meredith, and Melody Snelling. Forthcoming. *Absenteeism policies in Maryland middle schools*. Baltimore: Paragon.

- Arabic numerals are typically used for chapters, volumes, and other divisions.

- Ranges of numbers list the first and last numbers.

Books

- Tables and illustrations can use *fig.* for *figure*, but *plate, map*, and other illustration forms are spelled out.

N:	3. Chester R. Wilkins, *Classic Rock Bands: Their Influence on Contemporary Music* (New York: Parker Books, 2009), 74, fig. 2.1.

One Author, Editor, Compiler, or Translator

N:	1. Hector Cargill, *Hidden Tragedies of War* (Englewood Cliffs, NJ: Prentice Hall, 2009).
B:	Cargill, Hector. *Hidden Tragedies of War*. Englewood Cliffs, NJ: Prentice Hall, 2009.
P:	(Cargill 2009)
R:	Cargill, Hector. 2009. *Hidden tragedies of war*. Englewood Cliffs, NJ: Prentice Hall.

Two Authors, Editors, Compilers, or Translators

- Use *and* (not &) to separate authors.

N: 2. Cynthia Morgan and Anita Hantover, *Video Games: Good and Bad* (Defiance, OH: Orville Books, 2008).

B: Morgan, Cynthia, and Anita Hantover. *Video Games: Good and Bad.* Defiance, OH: Orville Books, 2008.

P: (Morgan and Hantover 2008)

R: Morgan, Cynthia, and Anita Hantover. 2008. *Video games: Good and bad.* Defiance, OH: Orville Books.

Three Authors, Editors, Compilers, or Translators

N: 3. Michael F. Brechteen, Pearl Karnel, and Roger M. Tingle, *Great Meat Packing Houses in the United States* (Chicago: University of Chicago Press, 2009).

B: Brechteen, Michael F., Pearl Karnel, and Roger M. Tingle. *Great Meat Packing Houses in the United States.* Chicago: University of Chicago Press, 2009.

P: (Brechteen, Karnel, and Tingle 2010)

R: Brechteen, Michael F., Pearl Karnel, and Roger M. Tingle. 2009. *Great meat packing houses in the United States.* Chicago: University of Chicago Press.

Books

More Than Three Authors, Editors, Compilers, or Translators

- Use *et al.* for footnotes, endnotes, and parenthetical citations.

- Do not use *et al.* for reference lists or bibliographies (list all authors regardless of the number).

N: 4. Jeremy Clintose et al., *Squirrel Hunting in Western Canada* (Baltimore: Pensacola Books, 2008).

B: Clintose, Jeremy, Richard L. Jaworski, Mitchell Pitt, and Peter K. Kowalski. *Squirrel Hunting in Western Canada.* Baltimore: Pensacola Books, 2008.

P: (Clintose et al. 2008)

> R: Clintose, Jeremy, Richard L. Jaworski, Mitchell
>   Pitt, and Peter K. Kowalski. 2008. *Squirrel*
>   *hunting in Western Canada.* Baltimore: Pensacola
>   Books.

Anonymous Works, Unknown Authors, or Works by Organizations

- List alphabetically by organization (if available) or title (ignore *A, An,* or *The*).

- When the author's name does not appear on the title page of the book, but authorship is known or assumed, then the author's name is listed in brackets with a question mark. Do not use the word *Anonymous* if the author's name is not known at all; simply begin the entry with the title.

Books

> N: 1. National Lung Association, *Organizations for Lung Cancer Survivors* (Philadelphia: National Lung Association, 2009), 27.

Authors' Names in Titles

- Omit the author's name and begin with the title for *footnotes* and *endnotes*.

- Include the author's name in bibliographies and reference lists (despite repetition).

- An example is an autobiography.

> N: 1. *Memoirs of Martin Klingert: An Autobiography*, ed. Charles T. Groves (Angola, NY: Branden Books, 2009).
>
> B: Klingert, Martin. *Memoirs of Martin Klingert: An Autobiography.* Edited by Charles T. Groves. Angola, NY: Branden Books, 2009.
>
> R: Klingert, Martin. 2009. *Memoirs of Martin Klingert: An autobiography.* Ed. Charles T. Groves. Angola, NY: Branden Books.

Editors, Compilers, or Translators in Addition to Authors

- List author, title, editor, compiler, or translator.
- *Edited by* can be listed as *ed.* (but not *eds.*), but spell out *edited by* in bibliographies.
- *Compiled by* can be listed at *comp.* (but not *comps.*), but spell out *compiled by* in bibliographies.
- *Translated by* can be listed as *trans.*, but spell out *translated by* in bibliographies.

N:	5. Karl R. Budenheim, *Modern Day Germany,* trans. Robert Handtmann (Cambridge, MA: Harvard University Press, 2008).
B:	Budenheim, Karl R. *Modern Day Germany.* Translated by Robert Handtmann. Cambridge, MA: Harvard University Press, 2008.
P:	(Budenheim 2008)
R:	Budenheim, Karl R. 2008. *Modern day Germany.* Trans. Robert Handtmann. Cambridge, MA: Harvard Univ. Press.

Books

Chapters in Books with One Author or Editor

- List author, chapter title (footnotes, endnotes, and bibliographies use quotation marks), book title (in italics), and page numbers or chapter.

N:	6. Charnel Heller, "The Color of Blue," in *Interior House Decoration* (Rehoboth Beach, DE: Pony Books, 2009), 221–43.
B:	Heller, Charnel. "The Color of Blue." Chap. 7 in *Interior House Decoration.* Rehoboth Beach, DE: Pony Books, 2009.
P:	(Heller 2009, 221–43)
R:	Heller, Charnel. 2009. The color of blue. In *Interior house decoration,* 221–43. Rehoboth Beach, DE: Pony Books.

Contributions to Books with More Than One Author or Editor

- List contributor, contribution title (footnotes, endnotes, and bibliographies use quotation marks), book title (in italics), authors or editors, and page numbers.
- This also applies to contributions at a conference.

N:	7. Bernard Woeber, and Harold Gilroy, "Nepotism and Promotion," in *Running a Successful Family Business,* ed. Alexander Hornung (Detroit: Dorfman Books, 2007), 12.
B:	Woeber, Bernard, and Harold Gilroy. "Nepotism and Promotion." In *Running a Successful Family Business,* edited by Alexander Hornung, 12–18. Detroit: Dorfman Books, 2007.
P:	(Woeber and Gilroy 2007, 12–18)
R:	Woeber, Bernard, and Harold Gilroy. 2007. Nepotism and promotion. In *Running a successful family business,* ed. Alexander Hornung, 12–18. Detroit: Dorfman Books.

Afterwords, Forewords, Introductions, or Prefaces by People other than the Author

- List afterword, foreword, introduction, or preface before the title of the book.

N:	8. Melchior Stemmer, forward to *Opening a Bump and Weld Shop*, by Theresa Van Mill (Chicago: Eschner, 2008).
B:	Stemmer, Melchior. Forward to *Opening a Bump and Weld Shop,* by Theresa Van Mill. Chicago: Eschner, 2008.
P:	(Stemmer 2008)
R:	Stemmer, Melchior. 2008. Forward to *Opening a bump and weld shop,* by Theresa Van Mill. Chicago: Eschner.

Non-Original or Secondary Sources

- If one source uses information from another, it is best to use the original to verify accuracy. However, if the original

source is not available, use "quoted in" to designate that
the original source was not used.

N:	1. Todd Morris, "Live and Let Live," *Rymes* 28 (May 2007): 122, quoted in Robert Travnell, *Poetry in Motion: Consider it Done* (Cambridge, MA: Harvard University Press, 2009), 83.

Editions

N:	9. Ralph Provesta, *Politics in the Deep South: The Struggle for Change in Established Venues*, 2rd ed. (Buffalo Grove, IL. Jones and Primmer, 2008).
B:	Provesta, Ralph. *Politics in the Deep South: The Struggle for Change in Established Venues*. 3rd ed. Buffalo Grove, IL. Jones and Primmer, 2008.
P:	(Provesta 2008)
R:	Provesta, Ralph. 2008. *Politics in the deep south. The struggle for change in established venues*. 3rd ed Buffalo Grove, IL: Jones and Primmer.

Books

Multi-Volumes

- Whole numbers are listed as arabic numerals.
- Omit the word *vol.* if the volume number is followed by a page number.
- When cited as whole volumes, list the total number of volumes after the title or editors' name.
- If published over several years, list the range of years.

N:	10. Erica Schnell, *Evolution of Polio Vaccination*, ed. James Heggles (Cincinnati: Cincinnati Books, 1991-99), 3:215.
B:	Schnell, Erica. *Evolution of Polio Vaccination*. Edited by James Heggles. 4 vols. Cincinnati: Cincinnati Books, 1991-99.
P:	(Schnell 1991-99, 3:215)

R:	Schnell, Erica. 1991-99. *Evolution of polio vaccination.* Ed. James Heggles. 4 vols. Cincinnati: Cincinnati Books.

Specific Volumes Cited in Multi-Volumes

- List specific volume (in italics), volume number, and general title (in italics).
- Use the abbreviation *vol.*
- Use arabic numbers for volume numbers.

N:	1. Katherine K. Mart, *Minor Miracles: The Lori Serra Prayer*, vol. 5 of *The Christian Tradition: A History of Spiritual Faith* (Center Line, MI: Superior Books, 1970), 9.

Series

Books

- Series titles are capitalized headline style (not in italics or quotation marks) for footnotes, endnotes, bibliographies, and reference lists.
- Series editors are typically omitted.
- Numbers (if available) follow the series title.

N:	11. Janine J. Remy, *Famous Mountains: The Himalayas,* Studies of Rugged Terrain 9 (Boston: Shackelford Books, 2009).
B:	Remy, Janine J. *Famous Mountains: The Himalayas.* Studies of Rugged Terrain 9. Boston: Shackelford Books, 2009.
P:	(Remy 2009)
R:	Remy, Janine J. 2009. *Famous mountains: The Himalayas.* Studies of Rugged Terrain 9. Boston: Shackelford Books.

Electronic Books

- Follow the guidelines for printed books.

- In addition to the full facts of publication, list the URL (after the publisher) and access date.
- Mediums other than the Internet should be noted.

N: 12. Chintu Moong, *Legal Documents Pertaining to Trade Agreements* (Bedford, TX: Legal Aid, 2007), http://www.legalaid.com/pubs/trade/htmlbook08/ (accessed November 23, 2008).

B: Moong, Chintu. *Legal Documents Pertaining to Trade Agreements*. Bedford, TX: Legal Aid, 2007. http://www.legalaid.com/pubs/trade/htmlbook08/ (accessed November 23, 2008).

P: (Moong 2007)

R: Moong, Chintu. 2007. *Legal documents pertaining to trade agreements*. Bedford, TX: Legal Aid, http://www.legalaid.com/pubs/trade/htmlbook08/ (accessed November 23, 2008).

Books

- Non-Internet sources list the medium or format (such as CD-ROM or DVD).

R: Baker, Thomas R. 2009. *Computer skills for beginners: Learning is easy*. Little Rock, AR: Clinton Books. CD-ROM.

Periodicals (Journals, Magazines, and Newspapers)

Periodicals

List Entries in the Following Order:

Authors – list editor if no author is listed

Article or column title – also list subtitle if applicable

Periodical title

Issue information – volume, issue number, date, etc.

Page number(s) – if applicable

URL (for Internet or other electronic sources)

In General

- Follow the guidelines in the *Books* section for listing authors or editors.

- Bibliographies and reference lists list the first and last page numbers of an article. Footnotes, endnotes, and parenthetical citations list specific article pages unless the entire article is cited.

- Article titles are capitalized headline style (in quotation marks) in footnotes, endnotes, and bibliographies. Article titles are capitalized sentence style in reference lists (quotation marks are not used).

Journals

Journals

- Journal titles are italicized and capitalized headline style in footnotes, endnotes, bibliographies, and reference lists.

- Journal titles are listed in full (omitting *The* if it is the first word in the title) in footnotes, endnotes, and bibliographies. Journal titles are often abbreviated in reference lists (especially for scientific works), but this is not mandatory. Abbreviations can be found in the *Periodical Title Abbreviations* (use an Internet search engine to find *Periodical Title Abbreviations*).

N:	1. Maxwell M. Anderson, and Bradford P. Wiltshire, "Obsolete Accounting Principles Revisited: Expanding the Role of the CPA," *Journal of Accounting Studies* 37 (2009): 147–53.
B:	Anderson, Maxwell M., and Bradford P. Wiltshire. "Obsolete Accounting Principles Revisited: Expanding the Role of the CPA." *Journal of Accounting Studies* 37 (2009): 147–53.
P:	(Anderson and Wiltshire 2009, 148)
R:	Anderson, Maxwell M., and Bradford P. Wiltshire. 2009. Obsolete accounting principles revisited: Expanding the role of the CPA. *Journal of Accounting Studies* 37:147–53.

- If page numbers follow a volume or issue, there is no space after the colon. However, if parenthetical information intervenes, then a space is placed after the colon.

No space before colon

Journal of Financial Research 17:221–34

Communication Research 16, no. 2:84–89

Space before between colon and pages

Communication Quarterly 23, no. 3 (Spring): 215–31

Sociological Review 13 (August 2001): 112–17

- Volume numbers are placed after journal titles using arabic numerals.

- Issue numbers in footnotes, endnotes, and bibliographies are placed after volume numbers (preceded by *no.*). Issue numbers in reference lists are placed in parentheses after the volume numbers (this is unnecessary when a month or season precedes the year). **Journals**

- Dates are placed in parentheses after volume numbers or issue numbers in footnotes, endnotes and bibliographies. Dates are placed after the author or editor in reference lists.

- Seasons are capitalized and are not necessary if issue numbers are listed.

N:	2. Darius R. Ricca, "Social Skills of Middle School Students in Advanced Math," *Education Quarterly* 21, no. 3 (2008): 215–31.
B:	Ricca, Darius R. "Social Skills of Middle School Students in Advanced Math." *Education Quarterly* 21, no. 3 (2008): 215–31.
P:	(Ricca 2008)
R:	Ricca, Darius R. 2008. Social skills of middle school students in advanced math. *Education Quarterly* 21 (3):215–31.

- Italicized terms within article titles remain italicized.

B:	Perez, Juanita J. "Health Concerns of *Shell-Shocked* Viet Nam Veterans." *Psychology Today* 21 (2007): 396–408.

- Quoted terms within article titles are placed in double quotation marks in reference lists and single quotation marks in footnotes, endnotes, and bibliographies.

B:	Mallinckrodt, Angela A. "The Influence of 'Dead Man Walking' on Death Row Inmates." *Communication Monographs* 12 (2008): 112–17.
R:	Mallinckrodt, Angela A. 2008. The influence of "Dead Man Walking" on death row inmates. *Communication Monographs* 12:112–17.

- Use *forthcoming* for works that have been accepted for publication in journals, but have not yet appeared. Position *forthcoming* in place of the year and page numbers. Capitalize *Forthcoming* in reference lists only.

Journals

N:	3. Kimberly T. Parrish, "The Relationship of Injury and Absenteeism in Produce Terminals: A Quantitative Study," *Journal of Human Resources* 19 (forthcoming).
B:	Parrish, Kimberly T. "The Relationship of Injury and Absenteeism in Produce Terminals: A Quantitative Study." *Journal of Human Resources* 19 (forthcoming).
P:	(Parrish, forthcoming)
R:	Parrish, Kimberly T. Forthcoming. The relationship of injury and absenteeism in produce terminals: A quantitative study. *Journal of Human Resources* 19.

- Unknown journals that might be confused with similar journals list the place or institution of publication in parentheses.

- Follow the guideline in the *books* section for listing editors, compilers, or translators in addition to authors.

B:	Hamby, Joseph T., ed. "The Influence of Lighting Levels on Consumption of Alcohol in Drinking Establishments." *Advanced Graduate Research Journal* (Central Michigan University Mt. Pleasant) 3 (2008): 23–34.

Scientific Articles from an Online Database

- Entries include the following (if available):

  Database name

  URL

  Descriptive phrase of locator -- for example an accession number or data marker

  Access date -- access dates are not listed in bibliographies for online databases

> N: 1, Pathogen Database, http://www.foodpath.db.edu (accession number FP0228364; accessed May 31, 2009).

Journal and News Articles from an Online Database

- Follow guidelines for printed periodicals.

- In addition to the full facts of publication, list the stable URL (which includes the name of the database consulted) and access date (access dates are not listed in bibliographies for online databases). **Journals**

> N: 2. Kachalk, Judith, "Paradise is Owning a Lawn and Garden Shop," *Macomb Daily*, July 22, 2008, second edition, http://www.mdn.homeandgarden/com/ (accessed March 31, 2009).

Electronic Journals

- These are journals found online, but not in a database.

- Follow the guidelines for printed journals.

- In addition, list the URL (after the publisher).

- List page numbers (if available).

- If page numbers are not available, add a descriptive locator (such as *under Work Related Stress* in the example below).

N: 4. Andrew W. Rosteck, "Situational Factors in Divorce," *Marriage and Counseling* 23 (2007), under "Work Related Stress," http://www.journal.uncc.edu/ mac/family/issues/t21/05924/05924.html (accessed May 4, 2009).

Magazines

- Follow many of the basic guidelines for journals.

- Cite by date (day, month, and year if available) even if issues or volumes are listed.

- Footnotes and endnotes list specific page numbers. However, ranges of pages (such as 23-45) are typically avoided since they are often widely separated by advertisements and other extraneous information.

Magazines

N: 1. Brenda Stickley, "Benefits of Teacher Job Sharing in Public Schools," *Education*, April 13, 2009, 37.

B: Stickley, Brenda. "Benefits of Teacher Job Sharing in Public Schools." *Education*, April 13, 2009.

P: (Stickley 2009)

R: Stickley, Brenda. 2009. Benefits of teacher job sharing in public schools. *Education*, April 13.

- Departments within magazines are capitalized headline style (without quotation marks).

N: 2. Alan Bellange, Alternative Musical Selections, *Hourly New Yorker*, December 1, 2009.

B: Bellange, Alan. Alternative Musical Selections. *Hourly New Yorker*, December 1, 2009.

- Departments without authors are capitalized headline style (without quotation marks) and listed by magazine.

P: (*Food Processing* 2007)

R: *Food Processing*. 2007. Food for Thought. May.

Online Magazines

- Follow the guidelines for printed magazines.
- In addition, list the URL (after the date) and access date.

Online Magazines

> N: 3. Maria Ellevich, "Macaroni Salad Extravaganza," *Food Preparation*, July 22, 2008, http://www. foodprep.com/salad/proc/issue/t33/33232.html (accessed January 2, 2009).
>
> B: Panobella, Stephen. "Small Musical Instrument Repair is Big Business." *Business Design*, May 19, 2007. http://www.busdesign.com/article/music/4225.html (accessed November 24, 2008).

- Page numbers are rarely available, but they are listed if found.

Newspapers

- Follow the basic guidelines for magazines, although newspaper articles may be omitted from bibliographies (the example in this book shows an article in a bibliography for demonstration purposes).
- Omit *The* from the beginning of newspaper names.
- Add cities even if the city is not part of the name (unless it is a well-known national paper).
- Add states (abbreviated and in parentheses) to unfamiliar cities.
- Add provinces (abbreviated) to unfamiliar Canadian cities.
- Add the cities (in parentheses) after names to foreign cities other than Canada.

Newspapers

The Boston Globe	should be	*Boston Globe*
The Gazette (from Baltimore, MD)	should be	*Baltimore Gazette*
The Wall Street Journal	should be	*Wall Street Journal*

The Bagley Press (from Bagley, Iowa)	should be	*Bagley (IA) Press*
Amory Times (from Amory, Mississippi)	should be	*Amory (MS) Times*
Herald (from London, England)	should be	*Herald (London)*

- Page numbers are typically omitted due to the potential number of editions that might be published in one day.

- Editions, section numbers, or other identifiers are listed (if available).

Newspapers

- Article titles in bibliographies, footnotes, and endnotes are capitalized headline style, and article titles in reference lists are capitalized sentence style. Convert article titles in full capital letters to uppercase and lowercase letters.

N:	1. Douglas Nolan, "Retail Sales Rebound on Strong December," *Detroit News,* May 31, 2008, late edition, sec. 1.
B:	Nolan, Douglas. "Retail Sales Rebound on Strong December." *Detroit News,* May 31, 2008, late edition, sec. 1.
P:	(Nolan 2008)
R:	Nolan, Douglas. 2008. Retail sales rebound on strong December. *Detroit News,* May 31, late edition, sec. 1.

Note: Newspaper citations are unique in one way. If all information is given in footnotes or endnotes, then corresponding entries are not necessary in bibliographies or reference lists (this is not required, but it is an option).

- Unsigned articles list the newspaper title first.

N:	2. *Montgomery (AL) Times,* "Red Cross responds to Hurricane Victims," June 12, 2007.

- *Letters to the editor* are treated generically.

> N: 2 Sharon Detmer, letter to the editor, *Boston Globe,* December 17, 2008.

- News service names are capitalized, but not italicized.

> 1.   4. Associated Press, "America's Gambling Addiction," *New York Times,* January 22, 2008.

Online Newspapers

- Follow the guidelines for printed newspapers.

- In addition, list the URL (after the date) and access date.

- Page numbers are rarely available, but they are listed if found.

- Descriptive locators are used (if available).

> B: Thomas Dittman, "Chicago Teens Gain Respect as Debaters." *Cincinnati Gazette,* March 15, 2008, http://www.cingaz.com/2008/march/youth/issues/ t31/94436.html (accessed June 20, 2009).

Reviews (of books, movies, plays, television shows, concerts, etc.)

List Entries in the Following Order:

> *Reviewer*
>
> *Review title* – if available
>
> *Work being reviewed*
>
> *Author, editor, directors, or translators* of work being reviewed
>
> *Location* – if a performance
>
> *Date of review* – if a performance
>
> *URL* – for Internet or other electronic sources
>
> *Periodical* – where the review appears
>
> *Periodical publication information* – if available

Book

N: 1. Denise Vickeroy, "New Perspectives in Focus Group Research," review of *Focus Groups: Reinventing the Wheel*, by Helen P. Davis, *Journal of Social Commentary* 10 (May 2008): 212–27.

Play

Reviews

N: 1. Watts, Charles, review of *Working Like a Dog: Our Long Journey*, by William Wyman, directed by Ronald Wood, Jagger-Richards Theater, London, *London Times*, October 17, 2009.

R: Watts, Charles. 2009. Review of *Working like a dog: Our long journey*, by William Wyman, directed by Ronald Wood. Jagger-Richards Theater, London. *London Times*. October 17,

- Unsigned reviews follow the guidelines for unsigned newspaper articles.

Interviews

- Best cited in footnotes or endnotes.

Interviews

List Entries in the Following Order:
*   Person being interviewed*
*   Interviewer*
*   Identifying information* – if available
*   Place of interview* – if available
*   Date of interview*
*   Accessibility* – if available

Unpublished Interviews

N: 1. Barry Gorlitz, interview by Connie Marston about the growth of Idaho high school basketball, Des Moines, May 21, 2009, tape recording, Idaho Sports Collection, Ashton, ID.

Unattributed Interviews (people who prefer to remain anonymous)

- The absence of a name needs to be explained in text (i.e. the interviewed person's name was withheld so current and future narcotics investigations would not be hindered).

Interviews

> N: 2. Interview with undercover narcotics officer, March 14, 2008.

Published Interviews

> N.   2. Retice Gould, interview by Edward Uddock, *Speaking Out*, CBS, February 4, 2009.

Personal Communication

- Best cited in footnotes or endnotes

Email

- Specific email addresses are not listed unless permission is obtained from the owner.

Personal
Communication

> N: 1. Peter Alphonse, email message to Rhonda Schneider, June 21, 2009.

Telephone

- Specific telephone numbers are not listed unless permission is obtained from the owner.

> N: 2. Malcolm Zheng, telephone conversation with the author, September 29, 2008.

Face-to-Face

> N: 3. Alyssa Jameson, personal communication with the author, January 26, 2008.

Unpublished Works

In General

- Material posted on the Internet is technically considered published. However, follow the guidelines for unpublished works when citing most posted Internet material.

- Titles are not italicized.

- Titles are capitalized headline style in quotation marks for footnotes, endnotes, and bibliographies. Titles are capitalized sentence style without quotation marks for reference lists.

<table>
<tr><td>N:</td><td>1. Scott C. Vandergeek, "Techniques for Snow Removal Equipment Repair" (computer printout, Department of Mechanical Engineering, Western Montana University, 2008).</td></tr>
<tr><td>R:</td><td>Vandergeek, Scott C. 2008. Techniques for snow removal equipment repair. Computer printout, Department of Mechanical Engineering, Western Montana Univ.</td></tr>
</table>

Unpublished Works

Dissertations and Theses

- List the author, title, type of thesis or dissertation (master's or PhD), academic institution, and date.

- The word *unpublished* is not needed.

<table>
<tr><td>N:</td><td>2. Dale M. Simko, "The Influence of Verbal Aggressiveness on Maintenance Personnel in a Manufacturing Environment" (master's thesis, Indiana State University, 2008), 132–34.</td></tr>
<tr><td>B:</td><td>Simko, Dale M. "The Influence of Verbal Aggressiveness on Maintenance Personnel in a Manufacturing Environment." Master's thesis, Indiana State University, 2008.</td></tr>
</table>

Lectures or Papers Presented at Meetings

- List the author, title, sponsor (organization, association, etc.), location (where the speech was given or paper was presented), and date.

- The word *unpublished* is not needed.

B: Cusmano, Andrea R. "Black Catholics in The United
      States." Paper presented at the annual meeting of
      the Council for University and Religion Dallas,
      TX, March 7-9, 2009.

Patents

- Cite under creator name and year of filing.

- Include patent number (if available).

R: Kitzman, Ken, and Corey Dexter. 2007. Exhaust
      noise reduction system, US Patent 5,495,326 filed
      Oct. 15, 2007, and issued Feb. 6, 2009.

Unpublished Works

Manuscripts

- List the title, date of item (list range if necessary), series title (if applicable), name of collection, and name and location of depository.

- For more detailed guidelines, follow *The Guide to the National Archives of the United States* (use an Internet search engine to find *The Guide to the National Archives of the United States*).

N: 3. Edward Cendrowski's Polish War Memoirs, 18
      May 1944, World War II Series, Warsaw Collection
      of Polish Manuscripts, Philadelphia Historical
      Archives, Pennsylvania.

B: Polish Manuscripts. Warsaw Collection. Philadelphia
      Historical Archives, Pennsylvania.

> N: 4. Minutes of the Committee for Ending Slavery, 1860-
> 1864, Papers of the New England Society for Slavery
> Abolition, Massachusetts Historical Archives, Boston.
>
> B: England Society for Slavery Abolition. Papers.
> Massachusetts Historical Archives, Boston.

Paintings, Photographs, Sculptures, and other Art

- List artist, title, creation date, and institution (if available).
- Italicize sculpture and painting titles.
- Place photograph titles in quotation marks.

> N: 1. Stephen Cortrellis, *Random Memories of Childhood Dreams*, 2007, Cleveland Art Museum.

Unpublished Works

Theater and Dance

- List title of work (in italics), key performers, venue, location, and date.
- List person's name first for individual performances with title in quotation marks.

> N: 1. *Heaven's Gates*, by Thomas T. Welch, directed by Martha M. Keller, Maryville Theater, San Francisco, June 14, 2009.
>
> N: 2. Dennis Williams, Guitarist, "La Vinca," by Maurice Rose, Orchestra Hall, New York, January 14, 2009.

Television Programs

- List program title (italicized), episode title, episode number (if available), venue (if available), date viewed, and original broadcast date.

> N: 1. *Little House on the Prairie*, "Laura's Horses," episode 29, October 4, CBS Classic Marathon, December 14, 2008 (originally aired November 14, 1974.

Electronic Mailing Lists

- List author (if available), name of list, date of posting, URL (if the list is archived online), and access date (if the list is retrieved online).

- Omit e-mail addresses.

> N: 5. Marcus Noullet, e-mail to Celiac mailing list, August 17, 2009, http://www.healthchanges.net/celiac/concerns/87334.html (accessed December 8, 2009).

Personal Web Sites

- Best cited in footnotes or endnotes (if used).

- List site name, title of site (in quotation marks), owner of cite, URL, and access date

> N: 7. Charles Ruffino's official Web site, "Musical Influences," Yolanda Ruffino, http://www.charles.ruffino.com/music/chat/88.html (accessed April 4, 2009).

Unpublished Works

Other Online Sources

- List author (if available), title of site (in quotation marks), owner of site, URL, and access date.

> N: 6. Angola Public Library Chief Financial Officer, "Agola Public Library 2008 Profit and Loss Statement," Angola Public Library, http://www.angolapublib.org/cfo/pandl/plan/99834.html (accessed August 15, 2009).

Special References

Dictionaries and Encyclopedias

Special Referen

- Reference books that are well known are generally cited in notes rather than bibliographies. Publication facts are not necessary, although the edition is required.

- List the title (italicized), edition (not volume and page numbers), and item (proceeded by *s.v.* [sub verbo]).

> N: 1. *Encyclopedia Britannica*, 14th ed., s.v. "Hemispheres."
>
> N: 2. *Dictionary of Modern Marvels*, 4th ed., s.v. "Airplanes."

Online Dictionaries and Encyclopedias

- Follow printed guidelines, but list URL and access date.

> N: 4. *Encyclopedia Britannica Online*, s.v. "Birds of Australia," http://search.eb.com/ bio/birds/ subjecttj5933.sci (accessed February 15, 2008).

Other Works

- List all publication details.

Special References

> N: 3. *Johnson's Handbook for Writers of Scientific Papers*, 5th ed., James Murphy (Boston: Scientific Research Association of America), 7.4.

Brochures, Pamphlets, and Reports

- List like books.

> N: 5. Gregory M. Kernacki, *Migratory Game Birds* (Warren, MI: Warren Tackle and Bait Shop, 2009).

Microform

- List like books, but also give page number (of printed text), fiche, frame, and row (if available).

> N: 6. Geraldine Willard, *Packaging Mythology in Forming Film* (Miami: University of Miami Press, 2008), text-fiche, p. 67, 5D14.

Abstracts

- List like journals, but add the word *abstract*.

> N: 7. Asmito, Karen A. "New Technologies in Heart Transplant Surgery," abstract, *American Journal of Medicine* 31, no. 3 (January 2009): 264.

Scriptural References

Christian or Jewish Scriptures

- List book (abbreviated), chapter, and verse (no page number).

> *For a chapter and verse in Luke (The New Testament)*
> N;   1. Lk. 12.3–21.
> P: (Lk. 12:3–21)
>
> *For a chapter and verse in Amos (Jewish Bible/The Old Testament)*
> N.   2. Am. 4:12.
> P: (Am. 4:12)

Versions of the Bible

- Work intended for general readers lists the version (at least on the first reference).

> *For a chapter and verse in James (The New Testament) from the New Revised Standard Version*
>
> N: 3. Jas. 4:13–16 (New Revised Standard Version).

Other Sacred Texts (i.e. Qur'an, Upanishads)

- Follow basic guidelines for other Christian or Jewish scriptures.

- More authoritative guidelines are found in the *History of Religions Journal* (use an Internet search engine to find *History of Religions Journal*).

Classical English Plays and Poems

- Typically list book, canto, and stanza.

> N: 1. Chaucer, "The Clerk's Prologue," *Canterbury Tales*, fragment 4, lines 7–49.

Musical Scores

Published Scores

- Follow basic guidelines for books.

> R: Mozart, Wolfgang Amadeus. 1956. *Sonatas and*
>   *fantasies for the piano.* Prepared from the
>   autographs and earliest printed sources by Jerry
>   Pokorny. Rev. ed. Fryeburg, ME: Landsford.

Audiovisual Materials

- Entries Include the Following (if available):

  Composer, writer, performer, or other primary person
  Title
  Recording company or publisher
  Recording identification number
  Medium (CD, audiocassette, etc.)
  Copyright date, production date, URL, or other helpful
  information – can be listed

Discographies

- List under a separate page titled *Discography.*

- For example, assume James Waterford is a Jazz musician (list titles in chronological order starting with the oldest).

> **1. Listing by Artist and Composition Titles**
>
> WATERFORD, JAMES
>
> "Walkin' Home," March 13, 1963. *My Life,* Blue Note
>   BST-67396.
>
> "Night in Harlem," January 14, 1964. *Holding a Hard Line,*
>   Blue Note BST-69665.
>
> "Living in Your World," May 12, 1966. *Liar's Breath,* Blue
>   Note BST-74503.

Musical Recordings

- Use for other than discographies.

N:	1. Jacob Wells, *Moonlight Blues*, Charity Records, Dolby HX TRC, Audiocassette.

Lectures or Readings (recordings of drama, prose, or poetry)

N:	2. Ibrahim Youssef, *Principles of Chemical Engineering*, audiotapes of lectures by Steven Hanisits and Edward Barth at the meeting of the Society for Chemical Engineers, Baltimore, January 14, 2008 (New Orleans: University of New Orleans Press, 2009).
N:	3. Kimberly Leeland, *Silver Wings,* performed by Peter Lambert and Scott Chandonette, Carriage Valley Records, CDLS-2008 (compact disc).

Audiovisual Materials

CD-ROMs or DVD-ROMs

- List the same as printed works.

B:	*American Standard Dictionary.* 4th ed. CD-ROM, version 3.0. Louisiana State University Press, 2007.
B:	*Complete Rolling Stone Magazine.* CD-ROM. Envision, 2008.

Filmstrips and Slides

N:	4. Eileen Harrison, *Gardens of Southern Michigan* (Williamston, MI: Gardener Education, 2009), slides.

Videos and DVDs

- List scenes (in DVD) following the guidelines for chapters in books.

N:	5. Sandra Devin, "Symbolic Spanish Gestures," *Cultural Meanings*, DVD, directed by Carlo Bautista (Santa Monica, CA: Sylvan Home Entertainment, 2009).

Legal Citations

In General

- Three different guides are acceptable for use, but for simplification purposes, *The ALWD Citation Manual: A Professional System of Citation* will be used for this book. For more in-depth detail on these guidelines, use an Internet search engine to find and order *The ALWD Citation Manual: A Professional System of Citation.*

- Italicize case names, titles of articles, titles of chapters, and uncommon non-English words or phrases.

- The publisher and place of publication are typically omitted, unless a book is reprinted or issued in a new edition with a different publisher.

- Omit periods from abbreviations of names that are recognizable. However, some abbreviations require periods.

> N: 1. *ACLU v. Burnell Sugar Co.*, 207 F.4e 361 n. 2 (9th Cir. 2009).

- Below are some examples of abbreviations that require periods.

v.	*is used for*	versus
n.	*is used for*	note
F.	*is used for*	Federal Reporter
F. Supp.	*is used for*	Federal Supplement
U.S.	*is used for*	United States Supreme Court Reporter
ch.	*is used for*	chapter
Cir	*is used for*	Circuit
ed.	*is used for*	editor or edition

Treaties

- Capitalize titles headline style.

- Use & instead of *and* to separate authors.

N:	2. Guillermo Diaz, & James Victor Crawford, *Federal Grants Laws for Small Business* ch. 10 (4th ed., Harkle Press 2009).
N:	3. "Biological Weapons Testing Ban," July 24, 2009, *United States Treaties and Other International Agreements* 29, pt. 4.

Chapters in Edited Books

- List the title of the chapter and the book (both are italicized).

- List the first page of the chapter and the specific page cited.

N:	3. Stacy Orlando, *Freedom of Information Act,* in *Law and Pubic Access* 112, 117 (Michele Miller ed., Runtle 2009).

Articles in Periodicals

- Well-known journals are abbreviated.

- List volume numbers in arabic (before the journal name).

- List the first page of the chapter and the specific page cited.

- List the date last (in parentheses).

N:	4. Kristen Osborne, *Verbal Aggression in The Courtroom,* 174 Yale L. J. 1263, 1275 (2008).

Legal Citations

Court Decisions or Cases

- Entries Include the Following (if available):
  Case names
  Volume number – in arabic
  Reporter series – abbreviated
  Ordinal series number – if applicable
  Abbreviated name of court and date – in parentheses

- List the opening page of the decision and the specific page cited.

> N: 5. *Theodore Crandle v. Jones Manufacturing*, 314 F.4d 245, 253 (7th Cir. 2009).

United States Supreme Court Decisions

- Published cases cite to *United States Supreme Court Reporter*. Not yet published cases cite to the *Supreme Court Reporter*.

> N: 6. *Kurlicci Meats v. USDA FSIS*, 621 U.S. 223 (2008).

Lower Federal Court Decisions

- Cite to the *Federal Reporter* or the *Federal Supplement*.

> N: 7. *Tonya Wikep v. EPA,* 191 F.304 (4th Cir. 2008).

State and Local Court Decisions

- Cite to the official state reporter.

> N: 8. *Helms v. Messner*, 92 Cal. 2d 856 (2008).

Constitutions

- List article, amendment numbers, and other subdivision numbers.

> N: 9. U.S. CONST. Art. VI, § 2.

Public Documents

In General

- Entries Include the Following (if available):

  Country, state, county, city, or other government entity issuing the document

  Executive department, legislative body, board, court bureau, committee, or commission

  Regional offices, subsidiary divisions, or similar

  Document or collection title – if available

  Author, editor, compiler, or translator – if available

  Report number – or other identifying information

  Publisher – if different from issuing body

  Date

  Page – if available

- Identify congress and session.

> N: 1. Senate Committee on Illegal Immigration, *The Immigration Act of 2008*, 114th Cong., 2d sess., 2008, S. Rep. 3246, 10–13.
>
> B: U.S. Congress. Senate. Committee on Illegal Immigration. *The Immigration Act of 2008*. 114th Cong., 2d sess., 2008. S. Rep. 3246.
>
> P: (U.S. Senate Committee 2008,10–13)
>
> R: U.S. Congress. Senate. Committee on Illegal Immigration. 2008. *The Immigration Act of 2008*. 114th Cong., 2d sess. S. Rep. 3246.

- Use 3-em dash for repeated references to the same congressional source.

> B: U.S. Congress. Senate. Committee on Global Warming. *Water Regulation...*
>
> ———. Committee on Global Warming. *Earth Changes...*
>
> ———. Committee on Global Warming. *Air Quality and...*

Documents and Reports

- Use *H.* For House and *S.* for Senate references.

- List Congress number, session number, and series number (if available).

> B: U.S. Congress. House. *Report on Food Security in USDA Inspected Poultry Slaughtering Facilities.* 110th Cong., 1st sess., 2008. H. Doc. 499.

Hearings (records of testimony before congressional committees)

- List titles.

> B: U.S. Congress. Senate. Committee on Endangered Species. *Wolves in the Southwestern United States: Hearing before the Committee on Endangered Species.* 112th Cong., 1st sess., March 23, 2009.

Resolutions and Bills

- Use *HR* for House of Representatives and *S* for Senate references.

- List title of bill, bill number, congressional session, and congressional record publication details (if available).

> N: 2. *Bank Reserve Act of 2006*, HR 2450, 101st Cong., 2d sess., *Congressional Record 212*, no. 154, daily ed. (November 25, 2006): H 8732.

Statutes and Public Laws

- Cite as statutes.

> N: 3. *Health and Welfare Reform Act of 2008,* Public Law 714–717, *U.S. Statutes at Large* 123 (2008): 71.

Municipal Ordinances and State Laws

- List the ordinance or law, the code, and the year the volume was supplemented or updated (along with a name, if available, to indicate the version of the code).

> N: 4. *Montana Rev. Code Ann* § 4129.34 (Hudson 2008).

Executive Department Documents

- Includes reports, circulars, and bulletins issued by bureaus and agencies.

- List authors (if available).

> N: 5. Timothy A. Wiechel, *Mutual Fund Investment for Upper and Middle Class Americans*, special report prepared at the request of the Department of Finance, March 2009, 27–29.

Census Bureau

- List bureau, title, and preparing division.

> N: 6. U.S. Bureau of the Census. *Median Household Income by State in the United States, 2008*. Prepared by the Housing Division, Bureau of the Census. Washington, DC, 2009.

Government Commissions

- Includes reports, circulars, and studies issued by commissions such as the SEC or FCC.

- List commission and title.

> B: U.S. Federal Communications Commission. *Annual Report of the Federal Communications Commission for the Fiscal Year*. Washington, DC: GPO, 2008.

Constitutions (Federal or State)

- List constitution, article or amendment, section, and clause (if applicable).

> N: 7. U.S. Constitution, art. 3, sec. 2, cl. 3.
>
> N: 8. U.S. Constitution, amend. 13, sec. 3.
>
> N: 9. Wyoming Constitution, art. 5, sec. 1.

State and Local Governments

- Follow guidelines for federal governments.

> N: 10. Missouri General Assembly, Tax Assessment
> Commission, *Report to the 95th General Assembly
> of the State of Missouri* (St. Louis, 2008), 12–17.

International Bodies

- Examples of acceptable abbreviations are listed below.

OPEC	*is used for*	Organization of Petroleum Exporting Countries
UN	*is used for*	United Nations
WTO	*is used for*	World Trade Organization
GATT	*is used for*	General Agreement on Tariffs and Trade

Public Documents

- List authorizing body (and author or editor if applicable), topic or title, date, series (if available), publication information (if available), and pages (if available).

> N: 11. R. M. Raines, "Chinese Trade Barriers to Western
> Countries," in *International Trade and Economy*, ed.
> B. Larson, chap. 6, Discussion Paper 174 (Geneva:
> WTO, 2008).

Online Public Documents

- Follow guidelines for printed documents.

- In addition to the full facts of publication, list the URL (after the publisher) and access date.

> N: 12. Michigan Constitution, art. 1, sec. 3, http://
> www.ligis.state.mi.us/ constitution/libry/terran24.
> html (accessed June 14, 2009).
>
> B: Michigan Constitution, art. 1, sec. 3. http://www.
> ligis.state.mi.us/constitution/libry/ terran24.html
> (accessed June 14, 2009).
>
> P: (Michigan Constitution)
>
> R: Michigan Constitution, art. 1, sec. 3. http://www.
> ligis.state.mi.us/constitution/libry/ terran24.html
> (accessed June 14, 2009).

Part Five
Sample Paper

Paper Setup
In General

- Use 8.5 x 11 inch paper (non-erasable type).

- Print on one side of the paper only.

- Use an easily readable font (i.e. 12 Point Times New Roman).

- The title is single spaced and centered in uppercase letters in the top third of the title page. If there is a subtitle, place a colon after the title and center the subtitle in uppercase letters on the following line (use single spacing).

- The author's name, course, date, and any other information required by the instructor are centered in upper and lowercase letters several lines below the title on the title page. Each piece of information is placed on a separate line with single spacing between.

- The title page is not numbered.

- Margins are one inch on all sides for the text, notes, bibliography, and references.

- Do not use full or right justification anywhere in the paper (use left justification only).

- Some universities require that the title be placed on the first page of the body of text. However, it is at the academic institution's discretion; the instructor should be consulted for specific guidelines.

- Double space the entire text portion of the document (with the exception of long quotations).

- Single space individual footnote and endnote entries with a double space between each entry.

- Indent the first line 3 spaces for footnote and endnote entries, and leave the following lines flush with the left margin.

- Single space individual bibliography and reference list entries with a double space between each entry.

- The first line is flush with the left margin for bibliography and reference list entries, and the following lines are indented 3 spaces (hanging indent).

- Use one space (not two) after punctuation at the end of sentences and after colons.

- Number pages consecutively with arabic numerals starting on the first page of text. The arabic numerals are listed flush right in the header.

- Indent paragraphs five spaces (using the tab key).

- Avoid hyphenating at the end of lines.

- Avoid underlining throughout the document.

- Indent long quotations (three or more lines of poetry or five or more lines of prose) five spaces (using the tab key) using single spacing. Quotation marks are not used for long quotations.

- Bibliographies and reference lists may include sources that were consulted, but not cited in the paper.

This Sample Paper utilizes the *notes-bibliography* source documentation system.

ORGANIZATIONAL ANATOMY:

Title

AN ANALYTICAL PERSPECTIVE

Subtitle

This page uses single spacing

Vladimir L. Kashnikov
Management Theory 455
December 14, 2009

Information required by Instructor

Erving Goffman's theory of self-presentation still ranks as pronounced sociological thinking. Essentially, his approach contends that life is a drama, which can be explained by individuals performing as actors on the stage of life. As actors, people present a different self to their audience based on the perceived salience of the social situation. The select information people divulge to others communicates how they wish to be treated in social situations and affects the approval and evaluation they receive in return.[1]

Goffman's reasoning is phenomenological because it integrates the complexities of socialization into something as simple as a theatrical production. He analyzes people's thought through processes and actions, and then demonstrates, through methodology understood by many, why they do what they do when they do it. Academic readers are often left "wondering why they did not come up with this idea . . . it could have made their careers much easier."[2]

This paper presents a theoretical analysis that is also quite rudimentary, asserting that the functionality of an organization can be elucidated by human anatomy. Specific departments in workplaces are viewed as anatomical divisions performing life-giving functions in an organization's metaphorical body. The discourse and action of the human composition define, shape, and change the organization. Image is developed as departmental synergy emerges and establishes organizational personification.

Survival of any organization requires a team effort from every department. This involves an influx of individuals, supplies, thoughts, and ideas.[3] The blood of an organization functions as a distribution agent for such essentials. People, materials, ideas, information, and technology flow through an institution for circulation to all body tissues. Blood is ubiquitous, flowing through all skeletal components and affecting every department. Without blood, the resulting intellectual and material deprivation would lead to breakdown and destruction of the organizational system.

The brain, vital to survival, functions as the CEO and major decision-making apparatus by processing information from other bodily components. Information is absorbed, evaluated and dispersed for implementation of strategies, policies, and procedures. Nothing is more important to the ultimate success of an organization than the actions of the brain, often thought to be the CEO of the operation.[4]

Like eyes and ears, management and marketing are key sensory advisors to the brain providing information for clarification, evaluation, and resolution of varied issues. Management individuals view the day-to-day operations of the internal organization, conveying their recommendations for growth and success. Without sight, the brain would be left blindly feeling around for information. Top managers often have the ability to see the organization as a whole rather than looking at individual pieces, which is why some people continuously climb the hierarchy ladder and others do not.[5] Marketing people hear what is being said outside of the organization and propose plans for prosperity in an ever-changing marketplace. Listening is not an innate aspect of humanity; it is a learned skill that is of significant importance for proper decision-making. Top marketers filter through all perceived sounds and find common themes for determining strategic recommendations.

Paraphrasing

The heart represents sales, which maintain and grow the organization. High blood pressure, equated with resistance to sales, can hinder and even stop the heart from delivering a free flow of blood and oxygen. Without the free flow of people, supplies, information, technology, and ideas, a slowdown or even shutdown of the system could result. A weakened heart due to age or neglect can also have devastating effects on the functioning or the life cycle of an organization. Exercise, in the form of education, training, and skill upgrades, is vital for keeping an organization mentally alert and healthy.

White blood cells in organizations are used for defense and maintenance. They repair, upkeep and upgrade the body so it can maintain peak performance. Education and training fall directly under the care of white blood cells, as does job skill development.

The liver acts as the quality assurance of the organizational body, constantly filtering impurities to meet product or service specifications. Process decontamination is critical for avoiding shortcuts and making sure procedures and specifications are properly followed. This cleansing reduces short-term thinking and aids the organization in long-run prosperity. Rarely, if ever, do organizations grow and prosper without the liver. One only needs to look at the rash of failed dotcom companies, whose products or services did not always keep pace with their escalating stock prices and paper net worth.[6]

Paraphrasing

Bones are the foundation from which the organization's principles are built. Every organization has a mission and purpose, and the bones provide the structure for that purpose. Bones strengthen to meet the needs or the body. Breaking a bone can result in losing sight of the organization's principles.

Only through a healing process can the bones regain the strength they once had.

The human skin is a protective outer layer that shields all internal organs. Like skin, public relations cover and protect all internal departments and are the first line of defense against attack from adversaries. Without an external covering, elements alone would wreak havoc on an organization's inner structure.

Public relations can work wonders for organizational image. Michelle Burtrise notes the following:

> Public corporations can boost their appeal to stockholders and stakeholders with positive image. Remember, however, that beauty may only be skin deep. False portrayal of image can be misleading and may even result in self-destruction. Turmoil, including financial disaster, can be occurring inside the organization while a rosy picture is painted on the outer shell. Case-in-points include the junk bond scandals of the 1980s. Bond purchases in these companies looked enticing to outside investors, but real net worth of these companies was grossly misrepresented and many individuals incurred substantial monetary losses, even to the extent of financial ruin.[7]

Two basic organizational motives are (1) to please members and (2) to please non-members. Members include employees and non-members include stockholders, customers, and the public. Image affects the evaluation the organization receives from members and non-members alike.[8] If, for example, a meat processing company were to publicly recall products adulterated with pathogenic bacteria due to unsanitary conditions, the public may not buy their products; stockholders may sell stock or demand explanations; and employees may look elsewhere for jobs. Similarly, an

Long quote (single spaced)

institution such as the American Cancer Society may lose supporters and members if the president is found to be embezzling money that was meant to go for research. Kenneth Morantz found that even small groups, such as a card club, may have a breakdown or reorganization if a member is found to be cheating.[9]

Organizational anatomy reveals an entity's presentation of self. Like the individual who performs on life's metaphorical stage, internal composition directly results in organizational performance on the world's allegorical rostrum. Through departmental interaction, an organization claims social attributes that describe its' particular public image.[10] This public image affects the evaluation the organization receives from members and non-members alike. While Goffman may have chosen a microcosmic view of the actions of individuals, organizations can be seen as much more complex structures in the same light.

Paraphrasing

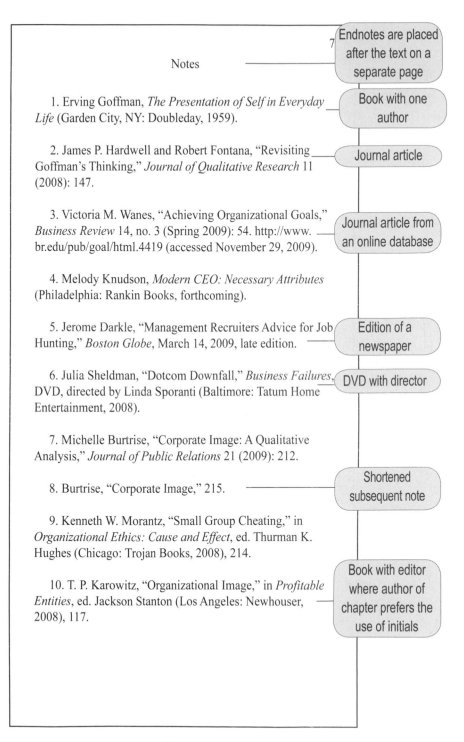

Notes — Endnotes are placed after the text on a separate page

1. Erving Goffman, *The Presentation of Self in Everyday Life* (Garden City, NY: Doubleday, 1959). — Book with one author

2. James P. Hardwell and Robert Fontana, "Revisiting Goffman's Thinking," *Journal of Qualitative Research* 11 (2008): 147. — Journal article

3. Victoria M. Wanes, "Achieving Organizational Goals," *Business Review* 14, no. 3 (Spring 2009): 54. http://www.br.edu/pub/goal/html.4419 (accessed November 29, 2009). — Journal article from an online database

4. Melody Knudson, *Modern CEO: Necessary Attributes* (Philadelphia: Rankin Books, forthcoming).

5. Jerome Darkle, "Management Recruiters Advice for Job Hunting," *Boston Globe*, March 14, 2009, late edition. — Edition of a newspaper

6. Julia Sheldman, "Dotcom Downfall," *Business Failures*, DVD, directed by Linda Sporanti (Baltimore: Tatum Home Entertainment, 2008). — DVD with director

7. Michelle Burtrise, "Corporate Image: A Qualitative Analysis," *Journal of Public Relations* 21 (2009): 212.

8. Burtrise, "Corporate Image," 215. — Shortened subsequent note

9. Kenneth W. Morantz, "Small Group Cheating," in *Organizational Ethics: Cause and Effect*, ed. Thurman K. Hughes (Chicago: Trojan Books, 2008), 214.

10. T. P. Karowitz, "Organizational Image," in *Profitable Entities*, ed. Jackson Stanton (Los Angeles: Newhouser, 2008), 117. — Book with editor where author of chapter prefers the use of initials

Bibliography is placed after the endnotes on a separate page

Newspaper article

Journal with two authors

Forthcoming book

Chapter in an edited book

Journal article from an online database

Bibliography

Burtrise, Michelle. "Corporate Image: A Qualitative Analysis." *Journal of Public Relations* 21 (2009): 211-218.

Darkle, Jerome. "Management Recruiters Advice for Job Hunting." *Boston Globe*, March 14, 2009, late edition.

Goffman, Erving. *The Presentation of Self in Everyday Life*. Garden City, NY: Doubleday, 1959.

Hardwell, James P., and Robert Fontana. "Revisiting Goffman's Thinking." *Journal of Qualitative Research* 11 (2008): 143-54.

Karowitz, T. P. "Organizational Image." In *Profitable Entities*, edited by Jackson Stanton, 112-19. Los Angeles: Newhouser, 2008.

Knudson, Melody. *Modern CEO: Necessary Attributes*. Philadelphia: Rankin Books, forthcoming.

Morantz, Kenneth W. "Small Group Cheating." Chap. 9 in *Organizational Ethics: Cause and Effect*, edited by Thurman K. Hughes, 201-28. Chicago: Trojan Books, 2008.

Sheldman, Julia. "Dotcom Downfall." *Business Failures*. DVD. Directed by Linda Sporanti. Baltimore: Tatum Home Entertainment, 2008.

Wanes, Victoria M. "Achieving Organizational Goals." *Business Review* 14, no. 3 (Spring 2009): 53-61. http://www.br.edu/pub/goal/html.4419 (accessed November 29, 2009).

Index

A

Abbreviations 25,
  27–30, 37, 49
Abstracts 86
Academic degrees 28
Academic designations
  20
Academic subjects 21
Afterwords 68
Agencies 29
Alignment 1, 2, 4
Annotated bibliographies
  53
Anonymous works 66
Art 84
Associations 21, 29
Audiovisual materials
  88, 89
Author-date system 41,
  42, 57

B

Bible 87
Bibliographies 42,
  52–56, 106
Bills 94
Block quotations 34
Books 22, 61–71, 105,
  106
Broadcasting companies
  29
Brochures 86

C

Canadian provinces 29
Captions 35
CD-ROMs 44, 89
Census Bureau 95
Centuries 25
Charts 37
Citation preparation 44
Citation styles 41, 42
Citing sources 33
Classical English plays
  and poems 87
Coding system 61

Colons 14, 15
Commas 13, 14
Company names 21, 29
Conferences 21
Constitutions 92, 95
Countries 29
Courses of study 21
Court decisions 92
Cultural terms 21

D

Dance 84
Dashes 15, 16
Databases 44, 75
Dates 25
Days 30
Dictionaries 85
Discographies 88
Dissertations 82
DVD-ROMs 89
DVDs 89, 105

E

Editions 69, 78
Editors 41, 43, 105
Electronic books 70
Electronic journals 75
Electronic mailing lists
  44, 85
Electronic sources 23,
  43
Ellipses 31
Email 81
Encyclopedias 85
Endnotes 42–51, 105
Ethnic, socioeconomic,
  and other groups 20
Exclamation points
  15, 34
Executive department
  documents 95

F

Figures 10
Filmstrips 89
Finding appropriate
  sources 7, 8

First drafts 8, 9
Font type and size 2, 4
Footnotes 42–51
Forewords 68
Fractions 24

G

Geographical terms 29
Government commis-
  sions 95
Graphic art 24
Graphs 37

H

Hanging indents 3, 5
Hearings 94
Historical and cultural
  terms 21, 22
Historical events 21

I

Ibid 33, 50
Illustrations 34–37
Inclusive numbers 27
Institutions 21
International bodies 96
Interviews 80, 81
Introductions 68

J

Journals 71–75, 105,
  106
Judicial divisions 26

L

Lectures 83, 89
Lecture series 21
Legal citations 90–92
Line spacing 1, 2

M

Magazines 71, 76
Manuscripts 83
Margins 1, 4
Microform 86
Military terms 22, 26
Months 30
Movies 23

Multiple authors 53, 59
Municipal ordinances 94
Musical recordings 89
Musical scores 88
Musical works 24

N

Names, personal 28
Newspapers 71, 77, 78,
    105, 106
Non-original sources 68
Notes and bibliography
    system 41, 44
Numbers 24–27

O

Online databases 75
Online dictionaries 86
Online encyclopedias 86
Online magazines 77
Online newspapers 79
Online public documents
    96
Online sources 23,
    43, 85
Organizations 20, 21, 29

P

Page numbering 3, 5
Paintings 24, 84
Pamphlets 86
Papers presented at meet-
    ings 83
Paper setup 97
Paragraph indentation
    2, 5
Paraphrasing 101, 102,
    104
Parentheses 16, 17
Parenthetical citations
    42, 43, 57, 58
Parenthetical notes 52
Patents 83
Percentages 25
Periodicals 22, 71
Periods 13
Permissions 36
Personal communica-
    tion 81

Personal names 19, 28
Personal web sites 85
Photographs 84
Physical quantities 24,
    25
Places of worship 26
Plagiarism 9, 10
Planning a document 7
Plays 22
Poems 22, 87
Prefaces 68
Public documents 93–96
Public laws 94
Punctuation 13–18
Punctuation marks
    Order of 19

Q

Question marks 15, 34
Quotations 30–34
Quotation marks 17,
    18, 31

R

Radio 23
Readings 89
References 52
Reference lists 42,
    57–60
Reports 86
Resolutions 94
Reviews 79, 80
Revising 11
Revolutions 22
Round numbers 24
Run-in quotations 30, 34

S

Sacred texts 87
Saints 29
Scientific articles 75
Scriptural references 87
Sculptures 24, 84
Secondary sources 68
Sections and subheadings
    32, 33
Semi-colons 14
Series 70
Set-off quotations 30

Signs and symbols 40
Slides 89
Social titles 28
Sources 34
Source citations 41
Source documentation
    systems 43
Source lines 36
Spacing 2
Special references 85, 86
Spelling 13
Sporting events 21
States 29
Statues 24
Statutes 94
Stub 38
Symbols 25, 40

T

Tables 10, 37–40
Television programs
    23, 84
Terms of respect 20
Theater 84
Theses 82
Three-or-four dot method
    31
Three dot method 31
Time designations 25,
    26, 30
Titles and offices 20
Titles of works 26

U

Unknown authors 66
Unpublished interviews
    80
Unpublished works 23,
    82–85

W

Wars 22
Web sites 44, 85
Works by organizations
    66
Works cited 52